EXPLORING WASHINGTON'S
Wild
Olympic Coast

EXPLORING WASHINGTON'S

Wild Olympic Coast

DAVID HOOPER

THE MOUNTAINEERS

7 6 5 4 3
5 4 3 2 1

Published by THE MOUNTAINEERS
1011 SW Klickitat Way, Seattle, Washington 98134

Published simultaneously in Canada by Douglas & McIntyre, Ltd., 1615 Venables Street, Vancouver, B.C. V5L 2H1

Published simultaneously in Great Britain by Cordee, 3a DeMontfort Street, Leicester, England, LE1 7HD

Manufactured in the United States of America

Edited by Miriam Bulmer
Maps by Vikki Leib
All photographs by the author unless otherwise noted. Photos on pages 57, 58, and 62 by Bob and Ira Spring
Book design by Bridget Culligan
Cover design and typesetting by The Mountaineers Books

Cover photograph: Ric Ergenbright/AllStock
Frontispiece: *Winter storms make mountainous seas*
Pages 10–11: *A great blue heron amongst gulls and other shorebirds*
Pages 50–51: *Watching for the whales*
Pages 84–85: *Hole-in-the Wall on Rialto Beach*

Library of Congress Cataloging in Publication Data

Hooper, David, 1946–
  Exploring the wild Olympic Coast / David Hooper.
    p. cm.
  Includes index.
  ISBN 0-89886-354-6
   1. Hiking--Washington (State)--Olympic Peninsula--Guidebooks.
  2. Olympic Peninsula (Wash.)--Guidebooks. I. Title.
  GV199.42.W220524 1993
  917.97'4--dc20   92-39552
                  CIP

Contents

The river is within us, the sea is all about us;
The sea is the land's edge also, the granite
Into which it reaches, the beaches where it tosses
Its hints of earlier and other creation:
The starfish, the horseshoe crab, the whale's backbone;
The pools where it offers to our curiosity
The more delicate algae and the sea anemone.
It tosses up our losses, the torn seine,
The shattered lobsterpot, the broken oar
And the gear of foreign dead men. The sea has many voices,
Many gods and many voices.

T. S. Eliot
from "The Dry Salvages"
The Four Quartets

Introduction

With the sharp seaward thrust of its schooner prow, the Olympic Peninsula is our continent's most prominent Pacific Rim landform, rivaled scenically and biologically only by Prince William Sound, pre-Exxon.

Like that beleaguered inlet, the Olympic Peninsula has suffered its own environmental ravages. Outside of the Olympic National Park (ONP), its old-growth forests have been plundered, its wild salmon face extinction—but within the park it remains in firm possession of its original collection of natural monuments: alpine glaciers, crystal lakes and streams, the best and biggest wilderness forest in the Lower Forty-eight.

And then there's the peninsula's wild and weatherbeaten western waterfront, America's longest untouched ocean coastline.

That rugged coast, a narrow seam between forest and sea, bears little geographic resemblance to California's smooth and sunny southern shoreline. Instead, it's more like that farther north, with sudden misty cliffs and conifered headlands punctuated by steep, secret beaches. Its prehistoric ramparts have been invaded by the sea, leaving ancient nearshore ruins: stubborn, surreal stone castles—sentinel sea stacks sprinkled with spruce and the nests of auklets. It is a broken sawblade of a coast, its battle with the sea one of violence and beauty.

Also unlike the beaches to the south, this rocky, rain-swept coastline teems with the creatures and plants of the sea and seashore, and the United Nations has officially designated it, along with the entire Olympic National Park, as a unique, invaluable, untouchable corner of the planet. Only at the prehistoric Indian fishing village of La Push and at the Kalaloch tourist village does civilization intrude.

Nature's reign extends offshore: the gray whales migrate through the protected seabird colonies on the offshore islands; they are no longer pursued by the coastal Indians in their long cedar canoes, but both Indians and canoes remain. Indeed, the native humans may be considered essential components of the ecology, so seamlessly did they fit themselves into it.

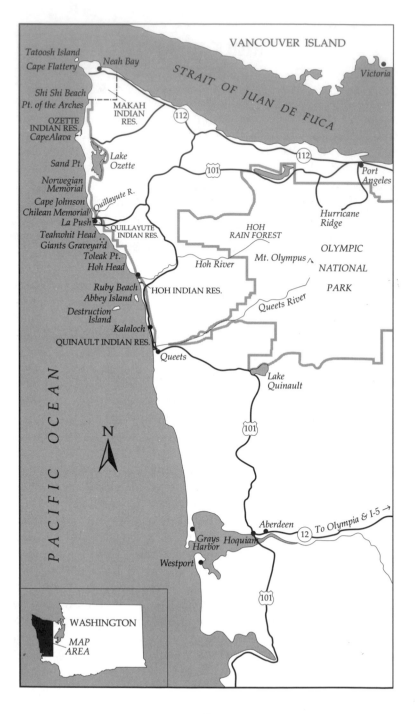

Despite the coast's wildness, it is accessible: motorists can see a bit of it through their windshields, casual hikers can reach much of it easily, and sturdy backpackers can walk its 60-mile length in a week or in weekend increments. The Olympic coast trailheads are at best a four-hour drive from the Puget Sound cities, the outdoorsy Northwest's largest enclave of trail walkers, and because of that distance this waterfront deals in that dearest of natural highs: total solitude, even in summer, when the ocean is calm.

In winter the gray North Pacific erupts into a rolling avalanche. The summer hikers depart and only a few meditative souls brave the gales to watch the thunder. Were it not for the world-famous mountains and rain forests nearby, fewer still would ever venture onto the coast's narrow access roads. Unlike many of this country's wild and beautiful places, it is hard to imagine this coast being overpopulated: it draws people who seek solitude, not the reassurance of other happy campers, people who must regularly trade the city's electric hum for the silent noise of Big Nature.

This book is for those people.

The "Exploring" in the title means exploration in an inner sense; the Indians had explored this seacoast thoroughly many thousands of years ago, but its pristine quality allows each of us to encounter it as though for the first time. It is an experience unique to wildland wandering: we encounter two distinct environments—the forest and the sea—simultaneously, but we observe them from their edges, a revealing perspective.

Like a hiking guide, this book details the terrain from Cape Flattery on the north to the Park's southern coastal boundary at the Queets River, preparing pedestrians for the unforeseen without spoiling the surprise, a commodity these rocks stock in volume. Like a nature book, this volume describes the coast's geology and its vibrant plants and animals, including the human.

Further, it offers the highland hiker some advice on seaside strolling, minor yet potentially lifesaving improvisations on the classic themes penned by packsacking's paternal pathfinders.

Mountain skills transfer easily, but hiking boots that have never tasted Olympic sea salt are not truly broken in, and their owners have yet to complete the course.

The Complete
Coastwalker's Companion

If, dear reader, you are not yet an experienced wildland wanderer, but your soul aches to be One with Nature, you are advised to do your homework. Join a hiking club, read books, buy the best gear you can afford, and resolve to spend as much of the remainder of your life as possible as far away as possible from the brain-numbing chaos that currently passes for civilization. But never chance any wilderness unprepared.

If you consider yourself versed in the pastime, but have limited yourself to exploration of the mountains or deserts, you'll be ready to negotiate the Olympic Coast as soon as you buy a good map and learn to read a tide table.

This chapter contains a collection of helpful hints garnered from many coastal treks, offered with as little repetition of the standard backpacking books as possible.

Many readers have already seen some of this coast. Those who have returned again and again know that it changes with every visit, revealing new secrets around every point, in every tide pool. Only the foolhardy think they know what goes on out here.

These backpackers forgot to unbuckle their waist belts before wading a creek.

What to Take

Beachwear

Clothing. Mark Twain correctly advised caution in approaching ventures that require new clothes. No problem. The experienced hiker will probably find an appropriate coastal wardrobe in the closet.

In summer, your clothing should prepare you for everything from cold evenings and mornings to sometimes-intense heat at midday. A winter hike demands the same warmth needed for cold-weather mountain travel, with special attention paid to staying dry.

Warm-weather hikers tempted to wear lightweight shorts should first consider how much protection they will provide while bottom-sliding over rock and drift logs.

At least some clothing should be kept dry inside tightly sealed plastic bags.

Headwear. Pack a wool cap, even in summer, plus a brimmed cap to cut sun and reflected glare from the rocks and water. Hooded outerwear provides extra protection.

Footwear. Bring thoroughly waterproofed hiking boots, plus a pair of sneakers for wading, tide-pooling, comfy campwear, and emergency back-up. (Boots are sometimes lost while hikers are wading barefoot or, when left overnight outside the tent, to mischievous deer.)

Caution: Vibram-type hiking boot soles slip easily on wet boardwalks and drift logs, and no known sole will provide good traction on moist or algae-covered rock. Walk with caution.

The blister-prone soon learn that traveling over rocky beaches is much harder on feet than smoother mountain trails, and sun-baked cobble can fry even the toughest tootsies. Treat your feet to a saltwater soaking whenever possible. Pack more socks than you ordinarily do. Winter hikers should wear gaiters to keep out sand and ambient moisture.

Gloves. Gloves are optional, but welcome on cold evenings and when using trail ropes.

Rainwear. Always be ready for rain. Ponchos snag on protruding branches more readily than rain pants and jackets and don't vent body heat very well, but ponchos usually cover the pack, make acceptable "beach blankets" on sunny days, and can protect your sleeping bag on tentless summer expeditions.

Skin and Eye Protection. Reflected ultraviolet rays from the ocean, rocks, and beach can cause sunburn, even on cold or partly cloudy days. Stiff winds can irritate eyes and lips. Carry appropriate medications. Sunglasses are a must year-round.

Hiking Sticks

Because of the rough terrain encountered on this coast, pedestrians—particularly those laden with heavy packs—may quickly come to regard a hiking stick as a near necessity.

Viewed either as a third leg or as an extension of the arm, a stick's value becomes most obvious when rounding a rough point strewn with boulders. Those without sticks are soon reduced to scrambling on all fours, while those properly equipped make speedier, safer, and more dignified progress.

You might find a nice straight driftwood branch at trailside or in the high-beach drift log piles, but don't count on it. A ski pole will serve (the sharp metal tip may skitter on rocks), but a hefty dowel from the lumber yard or a bamboo pole from the garden store are better. Outdoor shops stock pricey, ready-made sticks for the creatively impaired. An erstwhile mountain climber seen carrying his ice ax near the Chilean Memorial reported that it was a bit short to be a good hiking stick, but added he felt naked without it.

Your stick should be long enough to fit vertically under your armpit, or a bit longer. Crutch tips may be added to prevent undue wear and give added traction. Stylish wayfarers can add feathers, bells, and leather-lace handgrips; one bearded local wanderer has decorated his hiking stick with carvings that illustrate his travels and other personal-growth experiences, all of which he is willing to recite.

When rounding points, use your stick to scout footholds as well as to steady yourself. To cross horizontally from one boulder to another, poke the far rock to see if it's going to tip or if it's slick with wet algae. If all seems secure, put some weight on the stick and follow with one foot, then the other.

A hiking stick steadies a backpacker walking rough terrain.

When taking a long step down from one rock to another, let the stick support your weight until the leading foot makes secure contact. When ascending, "shorten" the stick by sliding your hand down the shaft.

On stretches of soft sand or rough cobble, the stick helps propel you forward as poles do in cross-country skiing; your arms can help your legs.

If you slip on the rocks, a quick stab with the stick may arrest your fall. If it doesn't, and you twist an ankle, the stick becomes a crutch, possibly getting you back to the car without having to leave your pack behind.

Sticks are also invaluable as probes when crossing streams and when wading around points where the bottom is vague and your footing can easily shift. A poke with the stick reveals the depth of the water and the firmness of the footing, and steadies you if it moves.

When you are ascending ropes, ladders, or very steep rocks and trails, the stick is best strapped to the pack so both hands are free. Do the same when descending, or just toss it to the bottom. It can also be used as a "rope" to pull a companion up a steep spot.

Sticks can prop up tarps and tents and, lashed together, can hold flashlights and water bags. They may be used to awaken sleeping companions from a safe distance, but should not be used to probe tide pools; the delicate organisms therein are easily damaged.

Packs

Given a choice, backpackers generally prefer internal-frame packs for coastal travel, simply because they don't sway as much as external frames and are thus less likely to throw a hiker off balance while rock-hopping.

Some mountain backpackers stack their external-frame packs to dizzying heights, a habit that may be reconsidered after crawling under downed beach-blocking trees, overhanging rocks, and dense trailside foliage.

Those opting for rain jackets rather than ponchos should bring waterproof pack covers.

Sleeping Bags

Protect your bag: if you get wet on a windy day, a dry sleeping bag might save your life. Before you stuff your sleeping bag into its stuff sack, push an open plastic garbage bag in first, then stuff your sleeping bag into the garbage bag and tie off the opening. The intensely paranoid can stuff this package into a second garbage bag.

It's a good idea to have a spare plastic garbage bag in your pack anyway; when all else fails, they make decent emergency shelters.

Equipment Maintenance

Everything gets exposed to sea salt, which can be very corrosive. When you get home, wash your pack, boots, and all metal gear (tent poles, cooking pots) with fresh water, even if they don't look dirty. Clean your camera and binoculars thoroughly, too.

Pets

Dogs are prohibited from the Olympic National Park coast, except on the beaches near Kalaloch and on Rialto Beach from the Quillayute River north to Hole-in-the-Wall, where they are allowed only on leashes. These restrictions do not apply to guide and hearing dogs.

Internal-frame packs are more stable when rounding rocky points.

Getting There

Driving

Assuming you're starting from one of the major Puget Sound cities, the most efficient way to reach the Olympic Coast is by car. In summer, traffic volumes swell considerably. Depending on where you're starting from and which coastal entry point you're headed for, the Olympic Coast trailheads are at least a four-hour drive from the major Puget Sound cities, while the trip to Neah Bay and Shi Shi Beach can easily consume six hours.

Highway 101 circles the Olympic Peninsula and offers you a choice of highway routes: the northern, via the ferries, through Port Angeles; and the southern, through Aberdeen and Hoquiam. Both routes include a lot of two-lane road, meaning a loaded logging truck or sedate RV can slow progress to a crawl.

The big slowdowns on the northern route are the highway traffic lights in Port Angeles and Sequim and the cross–Puget Sound ferries, which on warm weekends may require a several-hour wait. On the southern route, the long, slow tour through Aberdeen and Hoquiam can be tedious.

Car prowlers occasionally haunt the Olympic Coast trailhead parking lots. Leave nothing valuable in the car.

Official Entry Points

From north to south, the official entry points are Shi Shi Beach, via Neah Bay and the Portage Head trail; Cape Alava and Sand Point, via the Lake Ozette ranger station; Rialto Beach, via the Mora ranger station and campground; Second Beach, on the La Push Road; Third Beach, on the La Push Road; Oil City; and the many short trails along the "Destruction Island" section.

Unofficial Entry Points

The local loggers have been busy deforesting the woods behind the coast (the clear-cuts are less than a mile from the beach at some points), and their roads provide tempting alternative access routes. Some people use them.

"Target" signs like these mark the inland trail routes; some are hard to see in fog or dim light.

The ONP rangers advise hikers to use the official roads, parking areas, and trails. It's easy to get lost, both when hiking cross-country and driving, even for people who think they know the territory. Parked cars are sometimes vandalized.

The biggest hazard is the speeding logging trucks: the drivers aren't shy about running cars off the road.

Shuttles and Switches

Backpackers always try to figure out ways to avoid returning to the car the same way they came. With some prior planning, Olympic Coast hikers can reach the coast at one point and hike to the next exit point, thereby seeing much more of the coastline.

One way is to employ a shuttle driver. A few people who live in the western Olympic Peninsula area will, for a reasonable fee, meet you at a prearranged time and place, drop you off at your entry point, and then drive your car to your exit point, making their own arrangements to return to their homes. People who perform this service do so privately, not as employees of any business or of the ONP. Call the ranger stations for their names and telephone numbers.

You can also avoid doubling back by planning your trip with another party. Say, for instance, Party A agrees to backpack from Lake Ozette down to Rialto Beach, and Party B agrees to hike from Rialto up to Ozette. They can either hide spare keys in prearranged locations, plan on an exact time and place for an exchange somewhere in the middle, or leave the keys at the ranger station. The parties meet later and exchange cars.

A variation on the above plan calls for both parties to drive together to (in this case) Rialto Beach. Party A begins hiking north while Party B drives on up to Lake Ozette, then begins hiking south. The northbound party gets the keys en route and then comes back to meet the southbound party at Rialto Beach.

Lodgings and Campgrounds

Olympic National Park's coastal drive-in campgrounds are located at Lake Ozette, Mora, and Kalaloch. Numerous other campgrounds—both public and privately owned—are found throughout the western Olympic Peninsula area.

Rooms and cabins at La Push and Kalaloch are best reserved far in advance, even in winter months. Neah Bay's motels fill up quickly during salmon season; those in Forks usually have vacancies.

Call 1-800-942-4042 for information on motels and campgrounds in the western Olympic Peninsula area.

More information on accommodations is included within the appropriate "Coast Walks" chapters.

Currents, Waves, and Tides

*And over and through it all, the surf sound, here so
solid it seemed to have corners: the unremitting boom
on the seastacks, a constant crashing noise against
the shore northward. The surf. No other energy on the
planet approaches it. On any planet? The remorseless
hurl of it, impending, collapsing, upbuilding, and its
extent even beyond that of thunder, that grave enwrap-
ping beat upon all shores of all continents at once: how
is there any foothold left for us?*

Ivan Doig
The Sea Runners

In summer, high tides bring foot travel to a
halt at many points and headlands, just as highway construction stops
traffic. But the tidal delays are usually brief, and if no trail offers an alternate route over the tide-washed rocks, the hiker is allowed an hour
or two of relaxation on a nearby beach, where socks may be dried in
the sun and the sea's infinite mysteries may be pondered.

Winter hikers, however, will often have reason to ponder
Ivan Doig's poignant query: "How is there any foothold left for
us?" Not only are the tides higher then, but frequent storms stack
the incoming waves to such awesome heights that the beaches are
often awash, with two-ton drift logs bouncing about like bathtub
toys. At such times, coastal hiking presents unique challenges, and
is perhaps best compared to skiing in an avalanche zone.

To the casual visitor, currents, waves, and tides may seem to
be pieces of the same cake. But a little time spent living and walking at seaside reveals their differences: high waves can arrive at
low tide, and vice versa.

Currents

The ocean is not the continuous mass of water it appears;
the currents within it are like rivers within the sea, warmer
streams that flow in predictable courses.

The glass fishing-net floats and the Asian-labeled bottles we find on the coast were carried here by the Japan Current, which flows from north to south off the coast, speeding up and moving closer in summer.

A complex series of other currents move both north and south at different depths between the Japan Current and the Olympic Coast, including a wintertime plume of low-salt water from the Columbia River.

In summer, the wind tends to blow from the coast out to sea, moving the warmer surface water with it. The currents replace the warm surface water with colder, nutrient-rich water from the ocean depths, bearing food essential to the marine animals and plants that live near the surface and in the shoreline intertidal zone. Thus the wind and the currents combine to help create one of the richest, most productive marine habitats in America.

Waves

The difference between waves and tides lies in the forces that cause them. The pull of gravity from the moon and sun causes the tides to ebb and flow, but the ocean's waves are created by the friction of the wind blowing across the ocean's surface. The surf waves that wash these shores may have been born in mid-Pacific storms: the stronger the wind, the bigger the waves.

In summer, the sea off the Olympic Coast usually resembles a vast and serene lake. Although sea kayakers can testify that the summer surf packs plenty of power, it seems benign to the coastal hiker.

Winter unleashes Pacific storms that bash against the Olympic coast with as much or more power than any other shoreline in the world. Ocean scientists compare Olympic Coast conditions to those found in the treacherous North Sea: winds often gust close to (and sometimes above) one hundred miles per hour, and waves as tall as two-story houses (twenty-five— to thirty-footers are common) wash the beaches even at low tide. At high tide they toss more drift logs into their collections on the upper shoreline. These winter waves can quickly change the seascape: they bash the rocks with a force equaling two tons per square inch, and observers once watched as waves rolled a boulder estimated to weigh thirty-eight tons.

The storm clears, but giant waves still pound.

Foot travel is best delayed under such conditions; better to find a safe vantage point to watch the epic battle: Pacific Ocean versus Olympic Coast. At such times, moist sea spray and gray gloom pervade the atmosphere, obscuring the closest sea stacks, and the shorebirds take cover. The waterproofed observer, retreating to the stadium's upper deck, feels the vibrating thunder of the surf as it pounds the continental crust.

The storm may pass in a few hours. Sun shafts will pierce the clouds then, birds will resume their flights, but the waves may continue their onslaught, sometimes building even higher after the storm's end.

For some, an approaching storm cancels a coastal visit. For others, the ocean is never more majestic than when it is turbulent.

Tides

The ocean's tides are the most powerful natural force on earth, with cosmic powers continuously pulling the oceans to and fro across the planet. Earthquakes, volcanoes, and hurricanes are minuscule in comparison.

The moon influences the tides far more than any other factor. Many scientists believe it was torn from the earth billions of years ago when our planet was still a molten mass, leaving a depression now occupied by the Pacific Ocean. For a long time, the moon was so close to Earth it covered much of the sky, and its gravitational pull generated massive tides that dwarf today's.

But those tides gradually created a force counter to that of the moon, and, over the eons, the friction they generated by pushing against the earth's continents slowed our whirling planet like a finger rubbing against a spinning bicycle wheel. And that counterforce, which continues today, has pushed our moon 238,860 miles into space.

The sun's gravitational pull also influences the tides, but the moon is twice as powerful, because it's so much closer. The gravity field generated by the sun and moon produces a moving two-foot-high bulge in the ocean, one that becomes a high tide as it meets a shoreline. This bulge isn't the same as the swells mentioned in coastal weather reports; those are waves that move steadily without breaking.

Earthly forces also affect the tides, most notably the always-changing coastal weather. An approaching storm (usually from the south or southwest) will often lower the barometric air pressure on the ocean surface by an inch or more, often allowing the tides to rise more than a foot higher than predicted. The storm's onshore winds also contribute to a higher tide, which in turn pushes back rivers and streams, raising their levels. In winter, an approaching cold-air high-pressure system will sometimes produce very strong winds blowing offshore from the north, and these tend to lower the tide levels.

Other tidal influences include the centrifugal force of the spinning of the earth, the local geography, water depth, and the currents, among hundreds of other factors. Because of these differences, tides vary dramatically in different parts of the world. In Tahiti, they're hardly noticeable; in some coastal bays of eastern Canada, there can be a difference of up to sixty feet between low and high tides. Here, on this coast, the sea level varies by at least six feet a day and up to sixteen feet during the year.

The highest and lowest of tides—called *spring* tides—come about twice a month during full and new moons, when the moon and sun are in a straight line with Earth and can combine their gravitational forces. In the half-moon phase, when the three planets form a triangle, the forces of the sun and moon are weakest and produce the more-moderate *neap* tides.

Before and after: when high tides cover a point with no trail over the top, there's nothing to do but wait until the water recedes.

Prints of Tides: Understanding your Tide Tables

Rule: Do not venture far along this coast without having first consulted a tide table. This is crucial.

The rangers usually post a two-month tide table at the main entrance stations and at the unattended trailhead kiosks, but the supply is occasionally exhausted. To be safe, buy a one-year tide table booklet (about $1) at fishing supplies stores, marinas, and grocery stores near the coast (they're harder to find toward the end of summer). The local newspapers print a two-day tide schedule suitable for day-hikers.

If you're consulting a commercially printed table, first find the Pacific Beaches section and the table for the current month. Different publishers arrange the tables in slightly different ways: high tides are often bold-faced; minus tides (lower-than-normal low tides, which are great for tide-pooling) are often in red type.

The U.S. Commerce Department's computers reconcile the tide schedule with the calendar, and it is a complicated process. Because the lunar day is fifty minutes longer than the solar day, the tide schedule is continuously moving back, so that there are two unequal high tides and two unequal low tides during every *twenty-five–hour* period.

Therefore, every month, your tide table will list only three tides on some days, because the next high or low tide will occur after midnight on the following day. Notice that the higher of the high tides is usually followed by the lower of the two low tides, and the lower high tide is followed by the higher low tide.

When planning your hike, highlight the appropriate days' tides for quick reference. Coordinate each day's hike with the tides, noting where you might have to wait for a point to "dry out."

Of course, a tide table is all but useless without a watch. Some mountaineers declare their temporary freedom from civilization by leaving their watches at home. On the coast, keep it handy.

Maps

A good map of the ONP coast is almost as valuable as your tide table. It's hard to get truly lost on the coast, although some succeed: a couple of hikers heard a tsunami alert (a warning of a large wave caused by an undersea earthquake) several years ago near Cape Alava, panicked, and went crashing off into the forest, where they wandered around lost for three days.

Without a good map, it's easy to lose track of exactly where you are. That could result in mistaking an impassable point for one that could be rounded.

Consult the map at every rest stop and line up the major offshore islands with your changing position. Your compass (one of the Ten Essentials) will be of much more value in the mountains than on the coast, but is helpful for orienting yourself with the islands. Note how the larger rocks and islands appear to change in shape as you move along.

The best maps mark the points and headlands that are always impassable ("Danger" is a common warning), as well as those that usually become impassable with the rising tide. These points are usually marked "Caution," with a tidal height (expressed in feet above average water level) at which the tides probably prevent passage. If your map doesn't have these tidal heights for each point you'll have to round, ask a ranger for that information before you set out, and write it on the map.

For example, Cape Johnson is supposed to be roundable when the tide is less than four feet above average level. Your tide table might tell you that a seven-foot high tide is now in, which means you'll probably have to wait for it to drop about three feet, and will also tell you when the next low tide is expected. The map shows there's no trail over the top. Your watch will tell you about how long you'll have to wait.

A good map should also show where "high tide" trails pass over points and headlands. Look closely: some are very short.

Also, be aware that the ocean rearranges the furniture on an unpredictable basis; currents, tides, and storms alter the shape of the beach, thus no map can be accurate for long. And, as noted above, many factors—such as atmospheric pressure—can affect the tide and waves. Therefore, a point that *should* be passable, according to the map and tide table, may still be potentially hazardous. Several such small points aren't designated on any map, but are noted in this book's hiking guides.

Walking the Waterfront

The Olympic coastline presents the hiker with unique challenges and conditions. Only here does foot travel come to a halt when the twice-daily high tides block passage. Only here can a single mile of hiking traverse house-size boulders, then some slick ankle-twisting cobblestones, a deep stretch of boot-filling sand and a squishy swamp of kelp and seaweed, followed with a slippery wade through some cold surf.

These conditions may easily frustrate the organized hike planner, who sets daily mileage goals and schedules each successive campsite. Those accustomed to knocking off ten miles of smoother mountain trail may easily find themselves spent at the end of five miles of Olympic seacoast.

No secret technique can speed the pace on this terrain. No hiking secrets are offered here, but this: keep a steady rhythm in the stride as much as possible, one eye watching the rocks below, one cast upon the sea. That, and adopt a willingness to sleep wherever the sea and the rocks might assign you.

Points and Headlands

These sixty miles of northern Olympic coastline are a geologic sawblade, its teeth a ragged row of more than forty points or headlands, where hard rock formations have withstood the sea. Nature could easily have created a totally impassable coastline; that we can walk most of its length at seaside is a tribute to her providence. But the shoreline where these points and headlands meet the sea is rarely smooth. Between them, gratefully, lie softer coves and beaches.

Points usually slope into the ocean; headlands, or heads, are usually sheer-faced bluffs, some more than two hundred feet above sea level. The larger of these (Sand Point, Hoh Head) have been named; most remain anonymous.

Hikers can round most points and the smaller heads at water's edge at lower tide levels, and sometimes even at high tide.

A few big heads prevent passage at any tide level. Here, in most cases, trails lead up and over, as they do on many roundable points and heads, as alternate "high tide" routes. More about these trails follows.

Because the waves sort out a point's moraine of rocks, usually drawing the smallest to surf's edge and leaving the larger boulders up high, the point you breezed around at low tide could take much longer to round later at a slightly higher tide. A point you remember as being easily roundable may, on your next visit, be freshly sliced with a deep tidal surge channel. And one point's shaded north-side rocks may be coated with slimy algae that makes each step an adventure; the same area at the next point may be bone dry.

During stormy periods in winter, wind-driven high tides can make even the beaches impassable, effectively bringing all progress to a halt.

Rounding the Rough Spots

To round points and headlands covered with big, unstable boulders slickened with sea spray and algae, you'll have to shift down into scrambling gear and become a horizontal rock climber.

The path of least resistance—the lowest route through the smallest rocks—will usually be close to the water, but not always. Simultaneously, try to see as far ahead as possible, the next dozen steps or so, and the rocks directly underfoot. Every few steps, stop and check your route; you'll often see an easier one.

Review "Hiking Sticks" in the previous chapter. Those with no hiking stick will frequently find themselves grasping for nonexistent handrails. Stay balanced by maintaining at least three points of contact with the rocks, and test each new foothold.

Tighten the pack straps; a swinging pack can throw you off-balance. To descend from a high rock, take off your pack and then grab it from below.

Move slowly but steadily, at your own speed. The party should stay together in case of injury (expect minor scrapes on knees, elbows, and hands), but all should choose their own routes through the moraine. If fatigue sets in, regroup and take a break. Accidents are most likely when you're tired or moving too fast.

When high tides force the backpacker to climb a headland, a trail often becomes a dangling rope.

Rule: Never round a point on an incoming tide. You'll know you've made a mistake when you find first the route ahead and then your retreat blocked by incoming tidal surges and rocks too big to climb. Occasionally, hikers try to wade or swim their way out of these situations. Some do not succeed.

There are, of course, exceptions. If the map indicates that the point is small and the tide is not yet too high, pause for some planning. What about the next point? Where do you want to be when the tide is highest: the beach up ahead or the one just behind?

Let us, then, amend this rule: Never round a point on an incoming tide unless you are prepared to be stranded until the tide ebbs and you are certain of a dry sanctuary above the waves.

Trails Over Headlands

The only trails you'll encounter on this coast will be those leading to the beaches from the trailhead parking areas and those detouring over headlands. The former are mostly smooth and easy, allowing anyone who can walk a chance to see America's longest wilderness seacoast. The latter are not built for comfort.

All coastal trailheads are marked by orange-and-black "target" signs nailed to trees above the beach. They're easy to miss in dense fog or fading light.

The portions of the headland trails that climb from or descend to the beach are usually short but steep, sufficiently so to frequently require a secured rope or "sand ladder" (rungs of wood or steel joined by rope or cable), which should not be climbed by more than one hiker at a time. Where these climbing aids traverse bare slopes, hikers above can easily dislodge rocks, imperiling those below.

The going gets easier once the headland's summit is reached, although the trails are often very muddy, rough, and pass close to precipitous drops. Downed trees sometimes slow passage.

When conditions leave the hiker a choice, most will opt to round a point or headland at seaside, rather than climb over it. But the forest offers a cool respite from a hot beach and a soft umbrella against the wind and rain. The environment is lush, green, and quiet, a contrast to rocks and surf. And the views from above are magnificent.

Rivers and Creeks

Myriad freshwater streams—big rivers and tiny creeks—flow into the ocean all along this coastline's length, combining with the upwelling offshore currents to provide and circulate nourishment to the resident marine plants and animals.

In summer, hiking boots will allow you to slosh through or rock-hop almost all these streams without getting your socks wet, but two—the Ozette River and Goodman Creek—are sometimes unfordable. High tides and offshore storms push these streams back up into their banks, raising their levels, as do recent rains. Even in fair weather, these two streams should be waded as close to low tide as possible. Check with the rangers for current conditions.

The big, fast-flowing Quillayute and Hoh rivers are the only two watercourses that are *never* fordable. Both flow alongside Indian reservations, and you may be able to hire a powerboat owner to ferry you across. Otherwise, head inland to the highway bridges.

Wading

The coastal hiker will frequently find it necessary to wade a fast-flowing stream, a tidal surge channel, or a shallow spot off a rocky point; that, or turn back.

Wading always spices the trek with a little adventure, but should always be taken seriously: drownings are the leading cause of wilderness fatalities. And a false step in even shallow water can mean a thorough soaking, which, on a windy day, can lead to hypothermia.

Wading barefoot risks a cut foot; better to hang boots and socks around your neck or from the pack and change into sneakers, or wear your boots sockless (wet socks make great blisters).

In deep, fast-moving water, only one member of a party should be in the water at a time; the others should stand ready to assist. Loosen the pack straps, unbuckle the waist belt, and be ready to drop it should you slip and go under. You will not be arrested for removing your pants or shorts, thus keeping them dry for the march that lies ahead, and there is nothing quite so bracing as sloshing half-naked around a windy point on a cold day.

The best place to wade any sizable stream is the point at which it is slowest and shallowest. Often, the best place to cross a fast-moving beach creek is right at surf's edge, where the creek is much wider but relatively shallow. Check the other side to make sure you'll have an easy exit from the water, and look downstream to see where you'll end up if you're swept off your feet. Enter the water facing upstream and move sideways, using the hiking stick to help break the current.

Before wading off a point, watch at least a dozen incoming waves to judge their force. Toss a stick into the water to detect the direction and speed of any local currents. Look close for lurking (often barely submerged) drift logs, which can weigh a ton or more. While wading, keep watching the surf: larger "freak waves" can appear without much warning.

If you're swept off your feet by the waves, do not panic: survival is likely if you can stay calm. Get rid of your pack, then time your escape for the intervals between the waves. As waves approach, flatten yourself against any handy rock and hold on.

If you're pulled out into deeper water, swim between the waves, but do not try to swim against a current. If you get tired, tread water and float vertically, keeping your arms underwater and holding deep breaths in your lungs. Natural wave action should eventually push you toward the shore.

Correct wading technique in any water involves moving one foot at a time while keeping your weight on your hiking stick and the more secure foot, remembering that even big rocks can shift without warning. Probe the bottom continually.

If you hear a small voice inside your head telling you you're in danger, go back and think it over. Waiting is always safer than wading.

Coastal Camping

Some backpackers enjoy the camping more than the walking, and Olympic Coast camping is hard to beat: solitude, unbeatable views, a selection of tent spaces, usually plentiful water, abundant firewood, and a near-total absence of skeeters.

The coastal campgrounds administered by the Olympic National Park may be divided into three categories: the drive-in campgrounds at Lake Ozette, Mora, and Kalaloch, described in the appropriate chapters; the two hike-in campgrounds at Cape Alava and Sand Point, also described herein: both have outhouses, but few other amenities; and the hundreds of unmarked, undeveloped, first-come-first-served "tent spaces" that dot the beaches.

Most (but not all) beaches have at least one flat spot above the

A sunny beach camp well above the tide

tide line large enough for one tent, many can accommodate several tents, and some (like Rialto) can hold dozens. All such tent spaces are "natural"; they've never been cleared or leveled, but have simply developed over the years with repeated use. They are usually either a patch of level sand high on the beach, often buttressed with drift logs, or a clearing under the trees above the sand and logs.

All, without exception, are utterly charming. Evidence of previous habitation, if any, will almost always be limited to a rock-rimmed fire pit, some driftwood arranged as crude benches and tables, and perhaps a frayed "bear-bag" rope hanging from a nearby tree. Previous guests may leave notes in bottles.

On some beaches, you'll have a choice between camping under the trees or on the beach. If this is the case, let the weather decide. A forested site offers shelter from rain and wind, but big gusts sometimes bring down dead limbs. Exposed sites on the beach are colder at night, but catch the morning sun earlier.

Whenever you opt to pitch a tent on the sand, find the ragged line of moist kelp and seaweed left by the previous high tide, then check the tide table to see how the next high water will compare with the previous. Give yourself a healthy safety margin.

In winter or in stormy weather, it's safest to always camp back in the trees; the waves are unpredictable. Storm-season campers often hang another tarp or a surplus parachute to shelter the exposed campsite.

Tents

In summer, you can safely rely on a simple plastic tarp or a "bivvy sack" as a sleeping bag cover, as long as you can keep everything protected from sudden and unpredictable showers. The ONP's few remaining log shelters are damp and mouse-infested, and are intended for emergency use only.

Even when the weather's clear and warm, you'll often wake to find that a soft sea mist has dampened everything overnight. It's best to put your tent's rain fly on every night, no matter how clear the skies.

Most coastal backpackers carry tents year-round, and often bring a tarp to protect tent floors from the abrasive sand. Free-standing dome tents can be lifted and shaken to remove sand accumulations, and a small sponge and whisk broom will not go unused.

Before pitching a tent on the beach, find a straight piece of wood and smooth the sand flat, removing buried rocks and pieces of driftwood.

Long, fat tent pegs work best in sand, but still might pull out in a big wind; if so, tie your rain-fly lines to rocks or chunks of driftwood and bury them a foot deep.

Hammocks

Tent spaces above the beach often have adjacent trees standing at distances appropriate to the hanging of a hammock, and there is no better vantage point for the tedious tasks of wave watching and wildlife surveillance. Backyard hammocks may be too bulky for serious trekkers, but the flimsy-looking "backpacker" models roll up into a fist-size ball and are plenty strong enough for one person. Bring extra cord.

Campfires

Among the Northwest coastline's many claims to distinction is this: nowhere else in the world do the beaches accumulate permanent piles of drift logs. This is due to a unique combination of waterfront forest and onshore winds. The massive logjams lining the upper beaches were once trees in the interior woodlands; either through haphazard logging or floods, they fell into the coastal rivers and were swept out to sea, then blown back to shore by the waves.

The drift log berms remain as natural dikes against the winter storms, protecting the soft coastal forest soil from rapid erosion. They have their own rough beauty, and serve as homes for a variety of wildlife: chipmunks and river otters skitter through their inner sanctums. They provide visiting humans with sheltered beach camping and comfortable lounging.

And, almost always, they (or rather their attendant litter of broken parts) give us ample firewood—fuel for the flames that warm our bones, cook our food, and nourish our souls. One of the most enduring memories of camping on the coast is that of orange embers against a dark sea and a star-filled sky.

Campsites under the trees offer shade, shelter, and rustic furniture.

Nevertheless, there are times when the pleasures of a driftwood campfire must be or should be forgone. Always obey "No Fires" signs posted by the rangers during summer dry spells. Put out or modify your campfire if a stiff onshore breeze threatens to blow sparks back into the forest. Dry driftwood is scarce during or after rainy spells, particularly in winter, but you might find some under the drift logs. Fire starter or stove gas might get it burning; then more wood can be dried at fireside.

Driftwood is best gathered before nightfall. Do not cut live vegetation. Chain saws are prohibited. If there's an existing fire pit, use it. Dig out the sand the previous camper used to smother the fire. Collect any litter and burn it, if possible; if not, pack it out.

The ONP rangers require that campfires be at least ten feet from the nearest driftwood log (a log that catches fire may smoulder for weeks) and be three feet in diameter or smaller. Backpackers should always bring portable stoves, but you can cook on your fire if you bring a lightweight grill, which should be supported and well-balanced on rocks. Cobblestone-size rocks should completely encircle the fire.

On breezeless evenings, you may be pursued by the smoke from your campfire; the bulk of your body creates a vacuum that draws the smoke. A pile of rocks on the far side of the fire may pull the smoke in that direction.

Water

The ideal coastal camp lies adjacent to a cute little creek that emerges from the forest and cuts a swath across the beach to join the ocean.

Some beaches have no such streams; others have several. If you're planning a backpacking trip with overnight camps on specific beaches, don't assume that the creeks that appear on the maps as thin blue lines will still be there. The larger ones (those with names) will almost certainly still exist, but the smaller streams have a habit of drying up or changing course without notifying the mapmakers.

Be prepared to either adjust your plan or carry water to your campsite. In addition to one water bottle per person, your party could also carry a lightweight water bag, which, when full and when rough terrain must be walked, can be slung from a hiking stick draped across the shoulders or portered with a friend safari-style.

Because many beach streams cut deep beds in the sand, they may not be visible until you're quite close to them. Binoculars can aid your search: a flock of sea gulls on a distant beach is a 99 percent guarantee of a freshwater stream there. And a prominent pile of drift logs at a distant tree line will often have a creek flowing beneath; streams produce small bays in the shoreline that tend to calm the waves a bit, allowing logs and other debris to accumulate.

Not all coastal streams flow over the sand; some small trickles run *under* the beach. You can find their sources by walking back up into the forest and listening for their little gurgles and splashes. Look for wet spots, then trace them uphill. In extreme survival situations, water can sometimes be found by digging a shallow hole in the sand as high on the beach as possible.

The coastal creek water often has a distinctive brownish tea-like color given it by dissolved organic matter it's picked up while flowing through the forest. The water tastes just fine and is completely safe to drink, although it does seem to plug up hand-pump filters a little faster than mountain water. Treat, boil, or filter it as you would any backcountry water.

You may, on occasion, encounter brackish, slightly salty creek or river water (the Ozette River is often such), even at low tide. No treatment method will remove the taste. If distance or darkness prevents you from getting water from another stream, powdered drink mixes will probably save you from dehydration, and brackish water can be mixed half-and-half with fresh water when boiled for cooking purposes.

Food

The local raccoons will confiscate your rations unless you stuff all your food in a waterproof bag and suspend it from a line or tree limb near your camp. This procedure, often called "bear-bagging," should be followed at any campsite. Don't worry about bears on the coast: hunters have reduced the coastal black bear to

Raccoons are cute, but skilled at making off with backpackers' rations.

near-extinction, and they never threatened hikers when they lived here. If you're not sure how to hang your food, consult the rangers or a backpacking book.

Raccoons, when they're determined to get at a bear bag, can defeat almost any defense, perhaps even finding the other end of the line and biting through it. Take your food into your tent at night-only when no serviceable trees are evident, and don't be surprised if the raccoons try to rip a new door in your tent in the middle of the night.

The only alternative to bear-bagging is using wide-mouthed plastic jars with screw-on lids, available new or used (from restaurants, delis, or bulk-sale grocery stores). The raccoons may make off with even these, and will be further delighted if you leave your metal cookware outside the tent; a nightlong percussion ensemble will perform for your entertainment.

Raccoon are cute, and apparently some campers feed them. You'll usually see their bright little eyes about dinnertime, reflecting your campfire. They are also potentially dangerous; their sharp teeth and claws can do a lot of damage if they're angered, startled, or cornered. A chunk of driftwood tossed in their direction will usually convince them they should rely on their natural food sources, which are abundant.

And don't leave food lying around when you're away from the camp, even for a few minutes, even when no raccoons are visible. The ubiquitous crows are also smart and fearless, and skilled at making off with such items as large bags of chocolate-chip cookies intended to last an entire weekend. Mice will also enter an open but unguarded tent and can chew through wrappers.

Sanitation

Olympic coastal campers seem to be exceptionally conscientious. Almost always, garbage has been burned or packed out and evidence of human waste is nonexistent. The ONP rangers also work very hard at keeping the place clean.

The ONP has erected outhouses at various locations along the beach. Although they can become quite fragrant in summer, they should be used whenever possible. When no outhouse is within walking distance, it is still acceptable to head off into the forest with your toilet paper and trowel in hand, as long as you do your business (and dishwashing) at least one hundred feet away from the nearest stream. All human waste should be buried, but the forest soil here is often too dense for easy digging. If so, bury waste completely under fallen branches and rocks, and pack out your used toilet paper.

To soften human impact on the coastal environment, the ONP requires that hiking groups be limited to no more than twelve people. Larger parties should divide and camp a half mile apart.

Killer Garbage

Due to the vagaries of the currents, some beaches are almost completely free of washed-up litter, while others are strewn with plastic and rubber garbage. Its origins are primarily merchant ships, fishing boats, and naval vessels, which—although the practice is illegal—regularly dump at least six million tons of garbage annually (according to a now-outdated study) into the ocean to conserve on-board storage space. One recent study claimed that the coasts of Washington State and Japan have the heaviest concentrations of maritime garbage.

This junk is unsightly, and detracts from the wilderness experience. But, much worse, unknown thousands of seabirds and mammals (such as sea otters) swallow this floating garbage or are snared in it, and eventually die.

Hikers can help remove much of it. Before returning to the car, fill a plastic garbage bag with beach litter for disposal in the cans provided at the trailheads. Spend some time at each campsite collecting and piling garbage (weighted down with rocks and small logs so it won't be blown away) for retrieval by the rangers and civic groups that clean up beaches voluntarily.

The debris sometimes also includes steel barrels that hold or once held toxic chemical solutions. Don't touch these; they might still contain dangerous substances. Note an accurate location and any visible markings, and notify the rangers.

Side Trips

Bicycles

All vehicles, including bicycles, are prohibited from the ONP coastal beaches.

Swimming and Surfing

Comfortable ocean-beach swimming depends on warm water and a sandy bottom. The nearshore water temperature on this coast ranges from the low forties to the mid-fifties degrees Fahrenheit, too cold for most people. The bottom off most beaches is usually rocky.

Wading and swimming can also be hazardous. Currents are strong on some beaches, waves are unpredictable, and heavy drift logs threaten the unwary.

Surfers rarely venture out on this coast, mostly because of the cold water and rocky bottoms. In winter, conditions are too dangerous. Some practice the sport farther south, off the Westport beaches.

Photography

Serious photographers should brush their lenses continuously. Otherwise, fine sand will find its way onto the lens and into your photos. It even sneaks in under the lens cap. And salty spray will pervade both cameras and lenses, resulting in corrosion. Keep everything stowed away when not in use. Whenever you leave your camera on the tripod, slip a plastic bag over it. Clean everything thoroughly when you get home.

Secure camera gear when you're rounding rough points, and keep it off your chest when you're climbing or descending steep trails and ladders.

Bring a polarizing filter to subdue the glare off the water and to bring out the blue tones in the sky and sea.

Unless you're very lucky, you'll need an extra-long telephoto lens (400mm or longer; a 200mm isn't long enough) to "get close

A lone brave spruce clings to the summit of a doomed mini–sea stack.

to" the wildlife, such as seals basking on the offshore rocks. Such telephotos are expensive, but can be rented.

There's no surefire recipe for good seascape photography, but here are a few suggestions: The pros usually get their best shots at high tide. Waiting for a seabird to fly through the frame adds a sense of motion. Compose the elements of a scene, then wait for the right light. The sun casts its most dramatic illumination when it is low in the sky, either in the early morning or late evening. Getting a knockout midday photo is a real challenge, but it often pays to wait for a shaft of sunlight to poke through the storm clouds.

Boating

Kayaking off the open coast is for experts and strong advanced intermediates only, no matter what the weather or season. Smart sea kayakers wear helmets and wet suits, carry VHF radios,

Small-craft sailors usually find tranquil waters on Lake Ozette, but sudden storms can blow in from the ocean without warning.

and *always* travel in groups. If you're interested in coastal sea kayaking, join a club and get some experience.

Coastal travel in small open canoes is much more dangerous, but those with canoes will find happy paddling on Lake Ozette. See the "Ozette Triangle" chapter for more information.

Fishing and Shellfish

Almost all the good surf fishing lies within the southern Destruction Island section: Kalaloch, Beaches 4 and 6, and Ruby Beach are best. Some cast from the rocks just off Hole-in-the-Wall.

The catch is almost always surfperch, but sea bass may be hooked from rocky points at low tide. Local people net smelt from the beaches. Good baits for perch and bass include sand shrimp, clam necks, and nightcrawlers. It's illegal to use the tube worms found on the beach.

In any season, watch the waves closely for large swells and drift logs.

The rivers may yield salmon: spring chinook, steelhead, and silvers. Baits include sand shrimp, cluster eggs, and herring.

No license is required for fishing within the national park, but you must file a catch record at a ranger station or sporting goods store when you leave.

Shellfish harvesting—mostly of clams—is permitted on the ONP coast at some times. Be aware that eating shellfish that have been contaminated by toxic "red tide" algae can be fatal. Check with the ranger station for current regulations and conditions.

Beachcombing

No single beach within the ONP promises better pickings than any of the others; any may yield treasure on any given day. But experienced beachcombers know that the ocean cleans out its closets by combining a high tide with an onshore gale, and they note the direction of the wind and waves. A strong blow from the south, for instance, is more likely to leave fresh treasure on a south-facing beach than on one that faces west. And a treasure-barren summer beach might yield goodies in winter: near-shore currents change radically with the seasons.

The most prized items are the floating green glass balls lost

A Japanese glass fishing-net float hides in the kelp.

from Japanese fishing nets. They are rare and becoming increasingly valuable: the Japanese are converting to plastic floats, which are commonly found.

Such things as odd bottles with Asian labels and shreds of fishing nets are usually in evidence, but you're more likely to find interesting items of natural origin—keepsake seashells, exotic stones (those with "Swiss cheese" holes make nice candle holders), and odd-shaped driftwood.

The best finds are made when the beachcomber isn't really searching for anything, just letting the surfside kaleidoscope of shapes and colors soak in. Your pace should be slow, the path from eye to brain uncluttered.

Remember the good advice offered by Sir Isaac Newton, who scolded himself for wasting time by "now and then finding a smoother pebble or a prettier shell than ordinary, whilst the great ocean of truth lay all undiscovered before me."

He could have been referring to the strollers on the western Vancouver Island seacoast (a shore much like this one) who recently discovered a 17,000-year-old tooth of a prehistoric woolly mammoth. Or to the beachcombing schoolteacher who was the first to find the buried, ancient Makah village at Cape Alava in 1970, which had just been partially uncovered by high storm waves. That find was one of the most significant discoveries in North American anthropology.

There are more such out here, somewhere, waiting.

Emergencies

Backcountry Permits

These forms are posted at the trailhead kiosks, and are designed to alert the rangers to overdue hikers. All parties planning to camp on the coast overnight should fill one out, attaching the appropriate copy to one hiker's pack, where it should remain for the duration of the trip. Day-hikers are not required to do so, but should if they plan to venture a significant distance along the coast.

Bring a ballpoint pen, as well as some paper for emergency messages and poetic inspirations; the kiosk pencils are always dull.

Search and Rescue

Someone at home should know when you're expected to return, as well as your coastal entry and exit points. If you don't return when expected, that person should call the ONP (telephone numbers are listed below) and alert the rangers. Those returning late from hikes should make sure that the rangers will not begin an unnecessary search.

The phone numbers of the ONP Coastal Ranger Stations (area code 206) are: Lake Ozette, 963-2725; Mora, 374-5460; Kalaloch, 962-2283; and the ONP headquarters at Port Angeles, 456-4501.

Call 911 if these phones aren't answered. Hikers should carry quarters for pay phones.

Injuries and Illness

As in all wilderness areas, the burden of responsibility is on the visitor. Safety-conscious hikers are familiar with first-aid techniques, and normally travel with at least one companion. An injured solo hiker who is unable to walk may have to wait for days before another hiker happens by.

The rangers do patrol the coast, of course, but not on a predictable basis. "Rescue is not a sure or immediate service," notes an ONP brochure. "Be prepared to survive on your own."

If you report an injury, be able to pinpoint the victim's precise location. When notified of an injured, immobile hiker, the rangers may evacuate the victim via stretcher on the trails or, in extreme emergencies, by helicopter.

First-Aid Kits

A complete kit should be carried for even short day-hikes, but the most used items in it will be Band-Aids and disinfectant for cuts (barnacles and rocks), and an elastic bandage for knees and ankles twisted while walking on cobblestone. In hot weather, include salt tablets and sunscreen lotions.

Exposure

This is a common term for potentially fatal physical disability that occurs when the body gets either too hot (hyperthermia) or too cold (hypothermia).

Hyperthermia. Because the sand and rocks radiate the summer sun's heat, hikers (particulary those laden with heavy packs) can easily become seriously overheated. The first warning sign may be abnormal fatigue.

Hypothermia. Clothing soaked by rain or by a fall while wading—combined with wind chill—can lower the body temperature to sometimes fatal levels. The first warning signs may be stumbling and poor coordination.

Other warning signs and first-aid treatments for both hot- and cold-weather exposure may be found in books on general wilderness travel.

Tsunamis

Undersea earthquakes can result in large coastal waves called tsunamis, which should not be confused with storm-caused tidal waves. Although tsunami *warnings* are frequently issued, actual tsunamis are rare: the last to hit this coast with any force was produced by the 1964 Good Friday earthquake in Alaska.

Still, scientists say the coast is overdue for a large quake and a possible tsunami. Warn other hikers and head for high ground if you notice a sudden drop in the sea level, you feel an earthquake, or a coast guard helicopter flies over the beach broadcasting a tsu-

Cruising on a sandy carpet

nami or tidal wave warning. Don't return to the beach until the tide level returns to normal or when an "all clear" signal is given.

A Note About Safety

Safety is an important concern in all outdoor activities. No guidebook can alert you to every hazard or anticipate the limitations of every reader. Therefore, the descriptions of roads, trails, routes, and natural features in this book are not representations that a particular place or excursion will be safe for your party. When you follow any of the routes described in this book, you assume responsibility for your own safety. Under normal conditions, such excursions require the usual attention to traffic, road and trail conditions, weather, terrain, the capabilities of your party, and other factors. Keeping informed on current conditions and exercising common sense are the keys to a safe, enjoyable outing.

The Mountaineers

A Rock on the Wild Side

A Mountain from the Sea: The Creation of the Coast

The Pacific Ocean is encircled by a broken chain of volcanic vents—a constantly bubbling "ring of fire"—where the molten furnace inside our planet breaks through to the surface. Those we can see, like Mount St. Helens, erupt only occasionally.

But other volcanic vents lie offshore, on the ocean floor, and they "erupt" continuously. Those off the Olympic Coast (about 200 miles out) are part of a chain stretching from Oregon to Vancouver Island that scientists call the Juan de Fuca Ridge. From their visits in special research submarines, the scientists know these volcanic vents heat the surrounding seawater to 750 degrees Fahrenheit, warming a unique community of strange plants and creatures with heat from the inner Earth, not the sun.

Like other volcanic vents, these also pump up super-hot melted rock called magma, which cools and hardens when it meets the cold ocean, becoming the surface of a thirty-mile-thick layer of sea floor called the Oceanic Plate. More magma comes up behind the plate, and pushes it either west toward the open ocean or east toward the continent.

When the plate coming in from the ocean meets the Continental Plate, it is forced underneath and the two plates grind together, generating hot friction that produces more magma, which rises into (and occasionally erupts from) the inland mountain volcanoes.

Some fifty-five million years ago, when the Olympic Peninsula was about to be created, the volcanic vents were very close to what was then the continental coast, and they were much hotter. The planet was then almost four billion years old (the present-day human race is only about a million years old), and the continents had long been drifting about and changing their shapes.

The underwater vents gave birth to a huge mountain of magma, which forms the core of today's Olympic mountain range. Softer sedimentary rock, first washed out to sea from the continent, began to build up underneath the mountain of magma, and this combined glob of rock was slowly scraped off the Oceanic Plate and left on the Continental Plate's doorstep, much like mud from a boot: a mountain from the sea.

The Olympic Coast became the geologic equivalent of a bad multivehicle freeway accident—investigating scientists find sandstones, basalts, and breccias of vastly different ages and origins tangled together, crushed between the continent and the Oceanic Plate, their layers tilted at bizarre angles. Most is sedimentary rock, such as sandstone, but some is of volcanic origin; a few big chunks of basalt are visible in places like Second Beach south of La Push. When we scramble around the Point of the Arches, we're walking on 144-million-year-old pieces of the continent that were here before the magma mountain arrived, but, in comparison to the North American continent onto which it was joined, the Olympic Peninsula is still a very new place.

The sea level rose and fell several times, beginning the hydraulic blasting and carving that still continues, giving the

Sea stacks once were part of the continent; the ocean washes away the land in between.

Olympic Coast its distinctive hard headlands and sea stacks that alternate with softer beaches. The tabletopped offshore rocks we see today—Alexander Island, for example—were smoothed off by an earlier, higher sea level, one that reached a mile inland. The tops of other rocks were rounded.

The first of the most recent ice age glaciers arrived about two million years ago, and vast sheets of ice reached beyond the present coastline, covering the sea stacks and large rock outcroppings with a softer layer of rock carried along from as far away as Canada. The sea stack families—such as Point of the Arches and the Giants' Graveyard—were once buried by the glacial deposits, just as the Quateata headland just north of Second Beach is today, with its clearly visible layers of newer, looser rock covering the much older and harder sandstone.

Then, about thirteen thousand years ago, the global climate warmed, the glaciers began to melt away, and the first humans began crossing the Bering Strait. The melting ice raised the sea again, to about its present level.

The sea resumed its battle against the coastal rocks. The softer rocks surrendered quickly, becoming the beaches where we hike and camp today. About six thousand years ago, the bedrock bastion of Destruction Island was part of the mainland; the softer land between it and the present coastline has been washed away. But the harder rocks—the protruding points and headlands—are putting up a fight.

Their struggle is in vain. The waves attack like wolves circling a herd of caribou, concentrating their fiercest energy on the seaward tip of a rocky headland, charging from both sides. At each high tide they renew their assault, pushing air bubbles into tiny cracks in the massive headland, finding its weak points. Each blast of compressed air blows away a tiny fragment. Rocks and drift logs thrown up by the waves do more damage, as do the rain and wind.

Often the core of the headland's tip is the first to fall away, forming an arch; Hole-in-the-Wall, at the north end of Rialto Beach, is a perfect example. The arch, in a century or two, becomes a towering sea stack, now separated from its kin. The waves circle at its feet, gnawing and blasting, even as they themselves are chewed to frothy shreds by these fossiled teeth. Slowly, the tower disappears into the sea.

The rocks wage futile battle with the sea.

Turn-of-the-century pioneer photos provide a fast-forward glimpse of this erosion, showing coastal rock arches that are now piles of pebbles. In another century, our grandchildren will compare their coastline with the seascape photos we take today, and see further alterations. Several headlands—such as Hoh Head—may have seceded from the continent. Some offshore islands will have been swallowed by the sea and some of the beaches may be a football-field length farther inland.

Dramatic changes could occur very suddenly. The rubbing of the Oceanic Plate against the underside of the Continental Plate has mysteriously slowed, and although Cape Flattery still rises a tiny fraction of an inch every year and the peninsula's south-eastern corner drops a mite near Tacoma, scientists fear the two plates might be stuck against each other and might slip suddenly. If so, they say, the coast might be in for one of the most powerful earthquakes the world has ever known.

In a few moments, whole sections of coastline could drop several feet, creating a new shoreline. Headland cliffs might crash into the sea. An offshore earthquake could generate a tsunami that could take many lives, devastate coastal villages, and alter the sea-scape further. Scientists say evidence in the coastal soil suggests that huge tsunamis and earthquakes in the nine-point range (the worst possible) occur every four hundred to five hundred years, and that something similar to this scenario has happened rela-tively recently, about three hundred years ago. The Makah say a tsunami once temporarily turned Cape Flattery into an island (no approximate date is recorded), and many coastal residents remem-ber the sudden wave that hit the coast just after the Good Friday earthquake in Alaska in 1964.

But no earthquake could have greater impact than the tamperings of humans with the global climate. Our industries and oil spills have already weakened the coastal wildlife, and our gradual warming of the earth's atmosphere may someday turn the coast into a seaside desert. The plants and animals in the intertidal zone, for example, depend on a very narrow range of tempera-tures, and all life here is interrelated.

We come here to escape such worries. What we love about this coast is its timeless beauty, its permanence in an insecure world. But, considered against the coast's geologic history, that permanence is an illusion. The coast is chaos and change, the youngest addition to a new mountain only recently given us by the sea.

"A Bird Rock in the Blue Pacific"

Before dawn, long before the sun clears the forest and begins to light the sea, the seabirds begin to fly oceanward from their nests on the rocks offshore. Auklets, puffins, petrels—members of the Lower Forty-eight's largest seabird colony (with well over a quarter of a million birds by some scientists' estimates)—rise and race the sun to the sea, where they will skim the waves in search of food and then return to their nests on the Olympic Coast rocks at nightfall.

As the sun rises higher, more birds, other species, swoop along the beach and headlands, grazing the shoreline smorgasbord. A gull seizes a clamshell and shatters it on a rock from a hundred feet up. A dozen skittery sandpipers search for bugs in a drift of still-wet kelp and seaweed. Scoters—black sea ducks—bob in the swells, diving for small fish. A bald eagle swoops low, scanning the tide line, then ascends and perches on a ragged spruce snag.

Common murre

57

Cormorants

It is a tumultuous rendezvous of birds, of hundreds of different species. Some, like the eagle, live here all year; others—the auklets and puffins, among others—spend their winters in warmer climates. Some winter here and spend summers in the Arctic, and still more are simply passing through.

It is a beach built for birds, a wilderness for the winged. The fish-rich ocean is fed by clean rivers; its currents constantly push more nutrients to the surface. Equally important, the coast's 870 offshore rocks and sea-facing cliffs provide nesting places safe from four-footed predators; the seabirds fear only the scavenging gulls and eagles. The seabirds have designed wily ways to hide their eggs and young: rarely do birds dig tunnels into the earth, but several species—the auklets, puffins, and petrels—do so on the Olympic Coast's islands and sea stacks.

Humans damage the seabird populations much more than any natural predator, and in various ways. Hikers may occasionally see private airplanes buzzing the offshore rocks, even brazenly landing on the longer beaches. This is illegal—hikers should report the plane's fuselage number or at least a good description to the rangers—because one loud swoop can disrupt an entire nesting season.

While even more birds die ensnared in fishing nets and plastic garbage, oil spills are the seabirds' biggest hazard. Most of the spills are the frequent, relatively small slicks of waste petroleum dumped by passing ships. When seabirds come in contact with floating oil, they die quickly, usually because their oil-soaked feathers lose their insulating capability. Tens of thousands die when the coast is inundated with a catastrophic oil spill, like those that hit in 1988 and 1991.

But, remarkably, the Olympic Coast seabird populations remain strong, their off-coast homes protected from human harassment first as national wildlife refuges in 1907, then in 1970 as the Washington Islands Wilderness. In 1988, Congress designated thirty-four hundred square miles of the offshore waters as the Olympic Coast National Marine Sanctuary. At this writing, the sanctuary's boundaries and the question of what commercial activities might be permitted within them are still under discussion. See the Epilogue for more information on the sanctuary.

There is no better place than the Olympic Peninsula to practice the sport of bird-watching, or to learn it. All that's needed to begin are good binoculars and a North American bird-identification manual.

Novices soon learn that the best way to sort out the myriad bird species is by their choice of habitat, which fall into four basic groups: seabirds, shorebirds, water birds, and coastal forest birds.

The true seabirds, which live mostly on the offshore rocks and gather their food anywhere from close ashore to miles out in the ocean, include auklets, cormorants, northern fulmar, gulls (the California gull is most abundant), western grebe, pigeon guillemot, jaegers, kittiwake, loons, common murre, murrelets (the marbled murrelet was listed by the federal government as a threatened species in September 1992; environmentalists say the ancient murrelet should also be listed), brown pelican (endangered), petrels, phalaropes, tufted puffin, shearwaters (the sooty is by far the most abundant), skuas, and terns.

The shorebirds, which nest both onshore and off, feed mainly in the intertidal area and close to shore. They include dowitchers, dunlin, great blue heron, black oystercatcher, western snowy plover (considered endangered in this state), western sandpiper (the most abundant shorebird on this coast), surfbirds, turnstones, and the greater yellowlegs.

Water birds, most of which nest in the Arctic and Canada in spring or summer, feed close to shore. They include black brant (the world's smallest, fastest goose), sea ducks (scoters are most numerous), and the Canada goose.

The coastal forest birds, which rarely venture out beyond the offshore rocks, include bald eagles (listed as a threatened species by the federal government; there may be only 50 to 100 bald eagles remaining on the northern Olympic Coast. They eat mostly fish and some seabird young and eggs); crows and ravens; peregrine falcons (endangered); and kinglets, owls, thrushes, wrens, woodpeckers, and virtually all other forest birds common to the Northwest.

Less than a half-dozen scientific studies of the birds of the Olympic Coast wilderness have been published; much about them remains unknown. The first scientific naturalist to venture out to the offshore seabird rocks was William Leon Dawson, a self-taught bird expert, who courageously examined the auklet, puffin, and petrel rookeries with the aid of Quileute canoeists in 1906. The national seabird refuges were established soon after his Olympic Coast explorations, and his findings are revealed with wit and artful expression in *The Birds of Washington*, a rare, two-volume work published in 1909.

Dawson published other books about birds of other regions, but his readers may suspect the Olympic Coast was his favorite of all the places he explored. His love of these birds and their home often bursts from his otherwise-scientific accounts. ". . . [w]hat more romantic spot to charm the eye and fire the imagination," he declares, "than a bird rock in the blue Pacific!"

Whales and Whalers

The Plains Indians hunted the buffalo; the Indians of the Olympic Coast hunted the great gray whale. In both cases, it was something more than a simple quest for food.

The annual hunts for both whale and buffalo were woven into the tribes' social fabric. Each mammal held an important spiritual position in tribal culture and religion. In both cases, the primary hunters also held leading tribal roles. The hunts were well-organized group activities, but were always dangerous and often fatal to the hunters. The tribes used almost every part of both whale and buffalo for food, tools, or clothing. Proceeds of the hunt were shared throughout the tribe.

With the spread of white culture across America in the nineteenth century, commercial hunters reduced both buffalo and whale to near-extinction, just as racist government policy nearly wiped out the Native Americans.

But, in the latter part of this century, both the buffalo and the California gray whale—the species once hunted by the Olympic coastal Indians—have, through government protection, dramatically increased their numbers. Other whale species also frequent the coastal and offshore waters, but are much less numerous.

While the Quileute Indians of La Push and the Hoh River tribe engaged in whaling to some degree, the Makah—with five villages on the coast between Cape Alava and Neah Bay—were the recognized masters.

The Makah say that the gray whale literally shaped their society. The first members of the tribe to venture out on the ocean to hunt the whale became village chiefs and, generation after generation, their male descendants became both chiefs and the primary whale hunters, selecting other members of their eight-man crews from among their immediate families.

The crews pursued their quarry in thirty-six–foot whaling canoes, each cut from a single log. Before the canoe itself could be carved, it was necessary to "see" it inside the living tree; cedars that refused to reveal this image were left standing. As the tree fell to the ground, the cutters would turn away, so it could not see their faces. The tree might seek revenge for its demise, possibly by sinking in the ocean.

Pre-hunt rituals involved ceremonial fasting and bathing. The chosen eight would sleep together in a longhouse the night before the hunt, and some Makah say that the whalers' dreams foretold which whale would be taken.

At dawn, the whalers would leave the village. Their wives lay perfectly still during the whalers' absence, in hopes the hunt would likewise be peaceful. Finding whales, the hunters would approach soundlessly, with the chief firmly pushing (not throwing) the harpoon into the whale's shoulder.

California gray whale

Singing to the stricken whale, the crew would slow its flight with sealskin buoys and complete the kill with lances. The entire village would gather at the beach when the returning hunters were seen on the horizon, and would drag the whale ashore to be ceremoniously butchered.

About 1913 (the exact year differs in various reports), after the gray whale had nearly vanished, the coastal Indians voluntarily suspended their own traditional hunts until such time as the species could repopulate. A few tribal elders remember the whaling days, and a remarkable early photograph (taken by a Makah whaler) of a whale being harpooned, plus numerous whaling artifacts, are on display at the tribal museum in Neah Bay.

Following Federal protection granted in 1947, the most recent observations suggest that the grays have increased to near their original numbers (estimates range up to twenty-one thousand). They are the only whale specie to do so. Some Makah believe the whale hunting should be resumed, pointing out that some Eskimo tribes never ceased their hunts.

California Gray Whale

The Olympic Coast isn't the gray whale's home (although a few may linger about throughout the year); they migrate past here twice yearly, commuting between their Baja California breeding lagoons and their summer feeding grounds in the Arctic Ocean. This six-thousand-mile one-way swim is the longest migratory journey of any mammal.

The California gray whale (*Eschirichtius robustus*) is considered a primitive member of the whale family. Its ancestors actually walked on land about thirty million years ago. Adults are between thirty-six and fifty feet in length and weigh between sixteen and forty-five tons. They may live up to seventy years, but the average is thirty to forty years. When they surface, they can be identified by their mottled gray color and by their lack of a dorsal fin (common to most other whales); instead, they have a low hump and a series of bumps that are visible when they dive. They are often encrusted with barnacles.

Traveling day and night in groups of between two and twelve, they cruise at speeds of about four knots. They surface and "blow," or exhale, four or five times in a minute, then inhale a roomful of air and dive, remaining submerged for about four minutes, sucking in up to ten wheelbarrow-loads of bottom-dwelling crustaceans up to five hundred feet down.

Scientists are not universally optimistic about the future of the gray whale: intrusive whale-watching boaters, depletion of the fisheries, industrial pollution and offshore oil development all threaten its future security. Otherwise, the gray whale is harmed only (and probably rarely) by killer whales and large sharks.

Watching the Gray Whale

Few people can remain untouched by the experience of seeing whales moving through the ocean, by an inexplicable mixture of awe and tenderness for these huge, mystical mammals. But actually seeing them requires a combination of planning, patience, and luck.

Going to the right vantage point at the right time of year—and being prepared to wait a while—will almost always result in at least one sighting, and the gray whales sometimes come so close to shore to bottom-feed that you might fear they'll run aground. They rarely do, although they sometimes are washed ashore after dying at sea.

When to expect them. The whales head north between February and May, with March usually the month of best sightings. They then return south between late October and January, with November and December being the peak period. Some watchers claim the whales travel farther offshore in the fall, although this is not established fact. The six- to-eight-week migratory journey proceeds at a pace of about one hundred miles a day.

An ideal day for watching the whales is calm and slightly overcast. Rough water and the reflection of bright sunlight make it harder to see the whales when they surface. Watch for bushy "blows" up to fifteen feet high.

Be prepared for wind and rain at any time of the year. You'll want binoculars or a telescope, sunglasses, and a telephoto lens and tripod for the camera. Bring warm, waterproof clothing, sitting pads or portable chairs, a thermos for warm beverages, and maybe a small stove for hot meals and coffee. Take turns watching the ocean closely while others relax. Paperbacks, games, bird books, and kites help pass the time between sightings.

Watching for the whales

Where to see them. You might see gray whales at any time and place on the coast, as a few are thought to linger year-round, feeding at the mouths of rivers where food is especially abundant. There is no single spot where you're guaranteed to see whales, but they generally swim as straight north or south as possible, so they *usually* won't follow the curve of the coastline into a bay (but sometimes they do, occasionally into quite shallow water).

That means that the ideal viewing location is a headland that juts out into the ocean, one high above the water to give the greatest possible viewing range.

That's a good description of Cape Flattery, where whales often pass directly under the high cliffs. Portage Head, traversed on the way to Shi Shi Beach, has unmaintained trails to cliffs over the sea, and the high trails over the Point of the Arches area are also good bets, although these steep trails can be very slippery in wet weather.

Cape Alava reaches a good distance out into the ocean, but doesn't have much elevation. The nob at the tip of Sand Point gets you up higher. Easy boardwalk trails lead out to both points.

Teahwhit Head, between Second and Third beaches, and Hoh Head, about three miles north of Oil City, both offer excellent viewing, but getting out to cliffside involves a lot of bushwhacking.

The Destruction Island viewpoint north of Kalaloch on Highway 101 provides a wide and lofty field of view from the side of the highway.

Many people opt for the whale-watching charter boat excursions that depart from most coastal fishing ports. While the whales frequently come very close to these boats when the engines aren't running, marine biologists say that curious boaters frequently harrass the whales by motoring too close, sometimes causing them to change their migratory routes. Among other limitations, federal law stipulates that boaters not come within one hundred yards of whales, although whales often come very close to boats voluntarily.

If you decide to try a charter boat trip, be prepared for cold, wet weather in any season, as well as seasickness (take medication well before departure).

Life on the Rocks:
Introduction to Tide-Pooling

A separate province of nature lies between the forest and the sea, a unique collection of Lilliputian plants and animals, an ecosystem with a foot in both the marine and terrestrial worlds.

This narrow, fragile seam of life is called the intertidal area; most coasts have one, but these rocky shores boast the richest such habitat in both the northern and southern temperate zones. Offshore currents supply the Olympic Coast intertidal area with abundant food, and the moderate climate is neither too hot (fogs and clouds often shroud the summer sun) nor too cold (no killing freezes or shore-scraping ice).

It is a boisterous, bountiful biologic brew: numerous species of flora and fauna from both Alaska and California have found comfortable homes here, and this coastline, particularly its off-limits offshore islands, rival and even surpass lush tropical rain forests in biological wealth. And, as in those equatorial jungles, no niche goes unfilled by life in some form.

To marine biologists, this intertidal strip is a complex laboratory, a stage for experiments into the secrets of the ways of nature. It is one of the world's best such places, and there is much about it they have yet to fully understand, yet at least some intertidal rocks and tide pools are accessible to almost everyone. For the curious beach walker, these rocks can provide a wayside seminar in biology and a view through a well-washed window into wilderness.

The novice tide-pooler's first lesson is that the intertidal area is in delicate balance. Each species—some seven hundred different plants and animals thrive here between the lowest and highest tidemarks—works to ensure its own survival, yet also takes subtle, indirect measures to make sure its neighbors survive as well.

Examples are numerous. The usually orange sea star (or starfish), the largest intertidal resident, and the California mussel (perhaps the most numerous of the larger intertidal animals) stage an observable lesson in cooperative interaction.

Known as *Pisaster ochraceous* to the scientists, the sea star is a sheriff of sorts (with a badge for a body), assigned to keeping the California mussels (a big shellfish named *Mytilus californianus*) under control. If it weren't for the sea stars, the mussels would expand their thick beds (often covered with barnacles, on which the sea star also preys) to cover the entire central portion of the intertidal, simply shoving their neighbors aside.

The sea star lives in the lower part of the intertidal area, which is exposed only during the lowest of tides (the subtidal area below it is also rich in plant and animal life, but is never exposed). The lower intertidal is also the home of a variety of other animals, such as the purple sea urchins and the vivid green sea anemones.

But when the tide rises, the sea star slowly invades the mussels' mid-intertidal neighborhood, clinging to the rocks with its hundreds of tiny tube feet. Here, the tides flood and expose the rocks twice daily, meaning the resident plants and animals spend about half their lives underwater. In the natural world, such a lifestyle is unique.

Waiting to see a sea star move is the supreme measure of the boredom threshold, but films shown at high speed reveal that they wander about and seem to communicate with each other through tentacle touchings. When a sea star finds a mussel, it wraps itself around the shell and pries it open, inserts a part of its stomach to consume its prey, then, satiated, returns to the lower intertidal zone with the ebbing tide.

If the sea stars devour enough mussels, some two dozen other plant and animal species—especially barnacles and algae—can move in and spread out on the rocks. The fringe-topped anemone, which scientists believe can live to be one thousand years old, likes to settle near mussel beds, feeding on the scraps that ensue from the sea stars' feeding forays.

And the mussel beds themselves provide homes to some three hundred other smaller creatures, both here and higher on the rocks. The intertidal's uppermost limits are called the spray zone, where only the highest tides, surf spray, and rain moisten the rocks; barnacles and periwinkle snails are the most common resident animals. Between the spray zone and the mid-intertidal lies another distinct neighborhood, where the high tides submerge rock-dwelling whelks (snails) and limpets (a shellfish that eats algae), among others. Hermit crabs (who live in discarded snail

A tide-pooler makes friends with a purple beach crab.

shells) and tiny goggle-eyed fish called sculpins swim in the higher tide pools, mini-oceans that provide homes for plants and animals that can't live out of water.

Throughout the intertidal, hundreds of different plants—algaes, lichens and seaweeds, sponges, kelp, and several varieties of grasses—also play unique roles. As always, the plant life provides food and shelter for the animals, and, as elsewhere, the various plants compete with each other for scarce growing space on the rocks. But here in the intertidal, plants also struggle with animals for the limited available territory; on rocks exposed to heavy waves, for example, the sea palm (*Postelsia palmaeformis*) wages continuous turf battles with mussels and barnacles. In nature, this is rare indeed.

But amidst these little battles, a sophisticated network of interrelationships holds firm, guaranteeing that no single species can dominate for long, and that all will survive. It is an intricate plan: scientists generally believe that the beginnings of all terrestrial life probably gestated in some intertidal swamp three billion years ago, and the intertidal plants and animals have long since figured out secrets we humans, relative newcomers to this planet, can only study and attempt to understand.

Visiting the Intertidal Rocks

Think of an intertidal visit as a tour through a foreign country. It's possible to have fun without knowing anything about the place, but a little knowledge will make the visit much more enjoyable.

First, read a guidebook. Perhaps the most accessible is Anne Wertheim's book, *The Intertidal Wilderness*, published by Sierra Club Books, San Francisco; it has gorgeous photos and an insightful text. Check your bookstore or library for books by Thomas Carefoot, Eugene Kozloff, and Gloria Snively.

Come prepared. A tide table and watch are essential. A strong magnifying glass or hand-held microscope will reveal hard-to-see details mentioned in the books.

A low tide reveals intriguing plants and animals.

*Sea stars and anemone
await a rising tide.*

Sunny days call for a brimmed cap and glare-cutting sunglasses (serious photographers will need a polarizing filter). Seasoned tide-poolers wear fingerless gloves (sharp rocks and barnacles) and rubber boots (the ocean's near-shore Fahrenheit temperatures range from the low forties to the high fifties). Sneakers will suffice in warm weather, but don't go barefoot.

Where and when to go. Where depends on how far you want to hike. Lush intertidal grounds lie all along the ONP coast, and each is different. Usually, remote intertidal areas are healthier and more diverse. Those close to the highway in the southern section have suffered some trampling.

The intertidal is much more colorful in spring and summer, when tides are lower and big waves are less worrisome. Plan your trip around a good low tide; the lowest of the year are marked in the tide table with a minus sign. Hope for partly cloudy weather, as the sun's glare off the water can obscure your view into the shallow tide pools.

Getting started. Follow the ebbing tide, noting different species of plants and animals. Match them with photos in the guidebook (brought along in a plastic bag for protection).

Pause to read about what each animal eats and which intertidal neighborhood it lives in. Close inspection of a single tide pool or rock may reveal a dozen identifiable species.

When you've identified and studied several species, you'll start feeling more at home in this "foreign country." But don't be too scientific. Notice nature's artistry, too. Wertheim draws our attention to "images in color, form, and texture woven layer upon layer." The intertidal is a beautiful place.

Taking Safety Precautions

Know when the next high tide is due, keep an eye on your watch, and work your way back to the beach ahead of the rising waters.

Keep an eye peeled for large, unexpected waves, and for deadly floating logs in the surf. See the "Rounding the Rough Spots" section of "Walking the Waterfront" for tips on what to do if you're threatened by waves or trapped by the incoming tide.

Beware of hypothermia. Clothing soaked by rain or waves and chilled by the wind can lower your body temperature to sometimes-fatal levels. If your teeth start chattering, get warm and dry as soon as possible.

Take a complete first-aid kit and be ready to treat cuts from rocks and barnacles.

Using Intertidal Etiquette

Although these plants and animals endure and flourish against fearsome waves and weather, they're fragile and vulnerable to the careless ways of well-meaning humans. Behave as though you hope to be invited back again.

Limit your curiosity. Do not step on anything but bare rock. If you must pick up a rock to see what's underneath, replace it gently in the same position.

Don't poke the resident animals or pull them away from their resting places; you could easily injure or kill them. Nothing here bites or stings people. For the insatiably curious, *gentle* touching is permitted. If you gently place the underside of your forearm against a sea star's back and hold it there for a minute or so, it might (if it likes you) cling to your skin with its tiny feelers.

Don't even think about taking something home to put in the aquarium. It will die.

Footprints in the Sand: The People of the Coast

Only the Indians could find a foothold on this coast, and then only by truly becoming a part of it. Seafarers feared its rocks, loggers plundered its forests, settlers washed away in the tide of history.

Today, people argue over the Olympic Coast: should it be drilled for oil? Should its supporting forest ecosystem outside the ONP's thin coastline be further depleted? Or should the flimsy laws that now protect the coast's seaward and landward flanks be strengthened? All those issues pale next to the threat of global warming.

The Olympic Coast has endured in its present form for some fifty-five million years, but only in the last century has its natural beauty been damaged.

The First People

About twelve thousand years ago, the last Ice Age glaciers melted back from the coast, and nomadic Siberian hunters crossed the Bering Strait, perhaps venturing down along the coast in canoes while the glaciers were still close by. Some continued south and east, into the continent's interior. Some stayed.

Some nine thousand coastal people—part of a larger North Pacific civilization called the Nootka—divided into several tribes, among them the Makah, the Quileute, and the Quinault. The Makah lived in five villages between Neah Bay and Cape Alava, the Quileute at the mouths of the Quillayute River (a related tribe settled at the mouth of the Hoh River, and took that name), and the Quinault on the Queets River and farther south. (The two spellings of "Quileute" should be officially reconciled in favor of the tribe's version; that assigned to the river and the offshore wildlife sanctuary is generally considered to be European-American in origin.)

The Makah and the Quileute went out on the ocean in cedar log canoes to hunt whales. The ocean and the forest gave these people and the Quinault all the food they needed: salmon, clams,

deer and elk, halibut, and seal and sea lion. The cedar gave them
longhouses and clothing; the spruce, hemlock, yew, and maple
gave them baskets and medicine and fish traps. With plentiful
food, they had ample time to develop a sophisticated culture full
of song, ceremony, and tradition.

The Makah traded with Indians from across the Strait of Juan
de Fuca, from south along the coast, from Puget Sound on the east,

*The petroglyphs at Wedding Rocks include this outline of an
unknown tall-masted sailing ship.*

but their relations with the Quileute were not always amicable; each tribe raided the other's villages to capture slaves. When Makah war canoes appeared, the Quileute would often retreat to their high rock fortress atop James Island.

Other troubles were of natural origin, and left evidence in the coastal soil: at least one catastrophic forest fire roared up from the Columbia River all the way to Lake Ozette, and powerful offshore earthquakes apparently triggered tsunamis perhaps forty feet high that could easily have wiped out waterfront villages.

Close Encounters

History does not reach back to the day when the coastal Indians first learned that there were other people on this earth. Quileute and Makah legends reveal only that Asian sailors, probably storm-tossed fishermen carried east by the Japan Current, were washed up on these shores well before Columbus reached the Caribbean, as they have several times since. Some Indians still have tools made from the iron their ancestors salvaged from these shipwrecked vessels; the sailors became slaves.

Nor is the historical record clear on when the Indians first saw a tall-masted European vessel. Quileute legend tells of a group of white-skinned shipwreck victims who lingered with the tribe for many years until one day they set off walking to the south, never to return. A Greek named Apostolos Valerianos (also called Juan de Fuca) claimed to have explored the strait that now bears his name in 1592, after sailing north from the Spanish colony at Acapulco.

A common goal of all the Europeans who explored the Pacific Coast was to find a water route leading east to the Atlantic Ocean, the "Northwest Passage." The hazardous, harborless Olympic Coast was of little interest. While the Russians were offshore hunting sea otters from their Alaskan bases in the 1770s, the Spanish made regular visits to stake out territorial claims, and they are believed to be the first Europeans to land on this coast (at Point Grenville, south of the ONP, in 1775). British seafarers toured the area during the 1780s, but the Spanish solidified their claims in 1792 by building and occupying a small fort at Neah Bay for five months, becoming the first European settlers in what is now Washington State.

Relations between Europeans and Native Americans were troubled from the outset. Furs were traded for dry goods, but many early encounters were limited to warning shouts from the Indians and gunfire from the Europeans. The Hoh River was the scene of two tragic attempts to gather firewood and fresh water (by Spaniards in 1775 and British in 1786); rowboat crews were slaughtered on the beach, perhaps in retaliation for earlier offenses.

American Settlers

Although the Olympic Peninsula's interior was among the last American wilderness areas to be homesteaded, Americans established a trading post at Neah Bay and a lighthouse at Cape Flattery in the early 1850s. European territorial claims had been settled by the abdication of the Spanish and Russians, and by agreement between England and the United States on a Canadian-American boundary in 1845.

In the early 1850s, two-thirds of the Makah died in epidemics introduced by white newcomers, and the cultural memory that held much of the tribe's oral history died with them. Settlers began building homesteads on Quileute land at La Push in the 1860s, and, in an attempt to evict the tribe, torched the Indian village in 1889, destroying virtually all tribal artifacts from the precolonial era. Two years later, the settlers built a lighthouse on James Island, the Quileutes' high rock fortress. By some accounts, the island is named after the first white man who climbed it.

La Push's small river-mouth harbor made it a focal point for coastal commerce, mainly fur trading and delivery of supplies to homesteaders, who by then were also claiming land inland on the Hoh River and around Lake Ozette. The mail began to arrive every week in 1881, by canoe from Neah Bay when weather permitted, by foot-carriers along the coast when it didn't. One mailman played a flute as he walked, and claimed the curious seals would follow. There were no roads; the settlers drove cattle along the beach and ferried them up the rivers in small boats. At scattered locations along the coast, pioneer graffiti appears on bare rock faces: European names and turn-of-the-century dates.

Scandinavians, encouraged by the government's plans for a road and railway into the Lake Ozette wilderness, began a farming community there, one that grew to some 130 families. But their farms were included in the new Olympic Forest Reserve in 1897, and they began to move away, with timber companies buying up surrounding forestland made available by the reserve's boundary fluctuations. The long-promised road to the outside world was delayed until 1935, after almost all had left. Today, the only remaining evidence of the Scandinavian homesteads are names on the map: Lake Ozette's Tivoli Island; Ahlstrom's Prairie on the trail to Cape Alava.

Shipwrecks

Billions of dollars in lost ships and cargoes lie under water between the coast and the horizon—chests full of French gold may still lie buried off La Push—yet the sea washes the rocks clean, and few traces remain.

Although many ships vanished without verification on this coast before the nineteenth century, the first recorded shipwreck was that of the Russian fur-trading vessel *St. Nicholas*, run aground on Rialto Beach near James Island in 1808. Most of the crew was

Iron bolts and rotting timbers: the sea cleans out its closets.

ransomed after three years of enslavement.

The Norwegian Memorial at Kayostla Beach records the tragedy of the three-masted bark *Prince Arthur*. On a stormy night in 1903, its helmsman saw the light of a loggers' cabin and mistook it for the Tatoosh lighthouse. He turned east, and the ship was shattered on the rocks. Eighteen are buried under the stone memorial, wrapped in a sail from the doomed vessel.

The Chilean Memorial, just south of Cape Johnson, commemorates two shipwrecks, that of the *W. J. Pirrie* in 1920, with twenty drowned, and of the bark *Lenore* in 1883, with no record of victims.

Of the countless shipwrecked vessels themselves, only the rusted remains of the troopship *General M. C. Meigs*, cast up on the rocks below Portage Head in 1972 (with no loss of human life but some oil-spill damage to the tide-pool animals and plants), and an anchor from the *Austria*, wrecked off Cape Alava in 1887, can still be seen.

Defending the Coast

Japanese submarines were sighted off the Olympic Coast in the days following the Pearl Harbor attack in 1941. Fearing infiltration of spies and saboteurs, and even large-scale invasion, the military quickly organized a small coastal patrol force, with outposts at Lake Ozette, La Push, and Kalaloch. Supplemented by local militia and guard dogs, the patrols (first army and then coast guard) built shelters atop many headlands along the coast.

There is no official record of military contact, but rumors of infiltrating enemy saboteurs surfaced at least once. Some peninsula elders insist the military covered up certain incidents in the interest of national security. At any rate, the patrols reported they were exhausted and demoralized by their continuous, uneventful traverses of the strenuous coastal terrain, and pleaded for combat duty.

Oil, Gold, and Timber

Turn-of-the-century entrepreneurs wanted to see what was under the little pools of crude petroleum that bubbled up through the forest floor along the coast. They drilled first at the north end of Third Beach, losing a barge in the waves. The wildcatters fought with the boss, the equipment broke down, they found some oil, but not enough to continue. Another attempt was made in 1913, north of the Hoh River, and failed.

The big push to find oil came between 1931 and 1937, when eleven wells were sunk north of the Hoh. Realtors sold lots and built a collection of shacks they named Oil City. To attract investors, the oilmen promised a major discovery, one that was not forthcoming. The boomtown faded as fast as the oil, and few traces remain.

Drillers sank other unsuccessful wells along the Hoh in 1948 and 1965, both outside the present national park boundaries, apparently the last land-based explorations. The oil explorers then turned their efforts seaward, planting three exploratory platforms ten miles off Cape Flattery in the late 1960s. Again, satisfactory results were not forthcoming.

"Black gold" wasn't the only tantalizing resource on this coast. There are still thin traces of real gold here and there, and a placer miner named J. M. Starbuch found $5,000 worth, plus five ounces of platinum, while sifting the sands of Cedar Creek (about a mile south of the Norwegian Memorial) during World War I. Starbuch's mine played out by war's end, and his equipment now lies rusting back in the brush, but beach miners tended their sluice boxes (without noticeable profit) at other locations until the ONP took control in 1953.

While the coastal Indians cut a few cedars near their river-mouth villages to make canoes, baskets, and tools, most of the original shoreline forest was cut down around the turn of the century, when timber companies owned most of the land. The pioneer loggers hand-sawed the biggest, oldest trees—mostly western red cedar—and skidded the logs to the beaches with oxen, where at high tide the logs would be rafted off to the Grays Harbor sawmills.

But not all the trees were cut down; the environmental damage was not as severe as that inflicted by latter-day clear-cutters and, to the untrained eye, the coast's forest lining may appear virgin. To acquire the present swath of oceanfront, park officials traded inland old-growth acreage for the logging companies' second-growth coastal forests.

Little old-growth cedar remains on the coast and, since full-scale cutting began in the 1950s, it is rapidly disappearing from the public Olympic National Forest timberlands. After nearly a century of unmolested growth in a warm, wet climate, Sitka spruce (some are 200 feet high) now dominates the park's coastal forests, sharing space with the original biosystem of mosses, ferns, alder, cottonwood, and some larger species: Douglas fir, western hemlock, bigleaf maple, and shore pine.

All are tough specimens; those closest to the ocean are battered by high winds and sprayed by the sea's acidic salts. But, unless they are consumed by fire, the park's coastal forests might (in a few more centuries) once again be honored with the "old-growth" label, indicating a level of ecologic quality and diversity approaching that of the twelve-hundred-year-old cedars that once grew at surf's edge.

Saving the Seacoast

Environmentalists (then known as conservationists) realized early on that the Olympic Coast was a natural treasure, its spectacular scenery enriched by a diverse community of wildlife. William Leon Dawson, the first natural scientist to study the coast, catalogued its seabirds in 1906, and the offshore rock islands were officially designated as a refuge soon after.

A view of the coast north of "Lookout Point"

In the early 1930s, as paved roads penetrated deeper into the western Olympic Peninsula, arguments began to rage over how much protection should be given the mountain forests, the ocean coast, and their wildlife. As they do today, the area's logging and business interests advocated exploitation for profit; conservationists succeeded in convincing President Franklin D. Roosevelt (during a tour in 1937 that included the coast) that the peninsula's mountainous interior should be protected as a national park, and it was so designated (by one Senate vote) in 1938.

Roosevelt agreed with the conservationists that the ocean coast should be included in the park, but, against his wishes, the Senate excluded it. Through intricate and quasi-legal administrative maneuvering, he was able to withhold it from would-be developers, but not until 1953 was the present wilderness seacoast (minus the stretch from Shi Shi Beach to the Ozette River) officially included in the park by President Harry Truman.

Then the chamber of commerce forces renewed their campaign, calling (as they had previously) for a coast-hugging highway that would serve both tourists and loggers, one stretching from the Hoh River (where U.S. 101 now veers inland) to Cape Flattery, with numerous side roads that would allow motorists to drive on the beaches. The park's superintendent, a staunch ally of the loggers, shared their views.

But the conservationists rallied, with Supreme Court justice William O. Douglas as their leader, and in 1958 staged two media events—mass overnight hikes from Cape Alava to Rialto Beach—that drew a crowd of pro-highway sign carriers (one placard read BIRD-WATCHERS GO HOME), but stopped plans for the road's construction.

A decade after the Douglas hikes, backpacking's new popularity and the blooming of the environmental movement brought the Olympic Coast a fresh generation of admiring protectors. Novice coastwalkers sighed in sympathy as salt-sprayed pioneer packsackers recounted tales of bushwhacking trails over primeval headlands, but also told of a time (as recently as the late 1950s) when the tide-washed beaches, then owned by the state, were both a hunting ground for bear and sea lion and a place where loggers salvaged drift logs with bulldozers, all with the park's acquiescence.

By the end of the 1970s, the coast had slipped from the devel-

A hiker finds plentiful solitude and a seaward view on Third Beach.

opers' grasp. Its crown jewels—the Point of the Arches and Shi Shi Beach (as well as the coast south to the Ozette reservation and all of Lake Ozette)—were added to the ONP in 1977. In the mid-1980s, the park gained both the heretofore-overlooked intertidal zone and joint custody (with the U.S. Fish and Wildlife Service) of the offshore bird refuges; the Makah shot down a developer's plan to grace Shi Shi Beach with a tourist resort.

But petroleum prospectors had long been exploring off the Olympic Coast, and the oil companies—their cause supported by the Reagan and Bush administrations—proposed that the coastal waters be opened to offshore oil rigs. Although Congress, in 1988, created an Olympic Coast National Marine Sanctuary, its boundaries remain (at this writing) undetermined, as does the issue of whether it will include oil rigs.

Two major off-coast oil spills—one from a ruptured transport barge in 1988, another from a Japanese fish-processing ship that sank in 1991—have killed tens of thousands of sea-feeding birds and other wildlife, and coated virtually the entire coast in washed-up oil. A sanctuary with the largest-possible boundaries and the adoption of tougher international ship-safety rules might easily have prevented both catastrophes.

But after each spill, scores of volunteers—people who love the coast and its creatures—arrived unbidden to toil long hours at cleaning birds and beaches. When sheer exhaustion threatened to knock them off their feet, the arrival of another oil-soaked tide would draw them back to the polluted rocks; the arrival of another dying bird would always draw them back to the washing tables. If not for the unavoidable obligations of jobs and families, their numbers would have been multiplied a hundredfold. We can only hope that—as the history of the Olympic Coast unfolds into the future—the only footprints in these sands will be left by these people, those who hope to change the disastrous course of the last century's exploitations.

The Olympic Coast's environmental issues are discussed at greater length in the Epilogue.

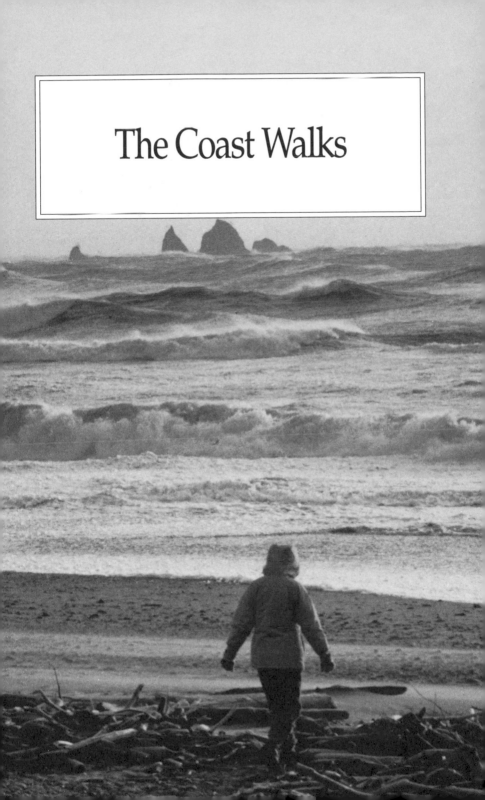

The Coast Walks

Walking a sea of tranquility

T*he following chapters* on hiking and back-packing the Olympic wilderness coastline all guide the reader *from north to south*, from a hike's first-mentioned point of oceanfront access to the point of exit. However, readers should rest assured there is no benefit gained or lost by reversing the north-to-south course described; the tides, the views, and the terrain will be equal in either direction. Those who do opt to walk the coast from south to north should read these chapters "backwards."

Many readers will not have the time or inclination to complete these long point-to-point treks (all but "Destruction Island" and "Ozette Triangle" will easily consume a three-day weekend), and will simply wander up or down the coast until it's time to turn around. Others can opt to shuttle cars from trailhead to trailhead as suggested in the "Getting There" chapter or simply arrange to have a ride waiting at their destinations.

The following are ten favorite places (listed from north to south) and can be considered a good introduction to the coast: Cape Flattery (an easy walk); Point of the Arches/Shi Shi Beach and "Shipwreck Cove"; Cape Alava/Wedding Rocks (an easy walk); Kayostla Beach; "Lookout Point," south of Starbuch Mine and due east of Carroll Island; Rialto Beach/Hole-in-the-Wall Rock (an easy walk); Second Beach (an easy walk); Toleak Point; Mosquito Creek; Ruby Beach/Abbey Island (an easy walk).

1.
Point of the Arches

SHI SHI BEACH TO THE OZETTE RIVER

Sooes Beach Trailhead to
Lake Ozette Ranger Station: *15.4 miles*

To reach Shi Shi Beach, follow the paved
main road west from Neah Bay, cross a concrete bridge on the left
over the Waatch River, and head south, watching for signs every
time the road branches. Take any road that promises to lead to
Sooes Beach, Shi Shi Beach, or the tribal salmon hatchery. Cross the
bridge over the Sooes River. Watch for road-hogging bovines.

Continue on (with the ocean on the right and homes on the
left) to a wide curve where a large sign points left to the hatchery.
The trail begins to the right of the sign. Park as far off the road as
possible. Vandalism is rare, but safe parking is available for a few
dollars a day at the homes back down the road.

Previous visitors fondly recall the old trail across Portage
Head to Shi Shi: a muddy, boot-sucking swamp first carved out
of the forest by the coast guard right after Pearl Harbor. At this
writing, the Makah are building a new version over the same 2-
mile-long route, one that promises dry hiking and environmental-
information signs along the way. As before, the new trail is mostly
level and shady; plan about an hour's walk from roadside to the
beach.

The tribe also plans to improve several side trails that lead off
to viewpoints high above the surf; safety fences will help prevent
falls. At present, finding the overgrown paths that lead to an old
military bunker and down to a rocky cove north of Shi Shi requires
some diligence.

Shi Shi Beach and the Point of the Arches
The trail abruptly opens high above Shi Shi Beach, with the
Point of the Arches dominating the southern seascape, and
branches at the backcountry registration kiosk (also the Makah/

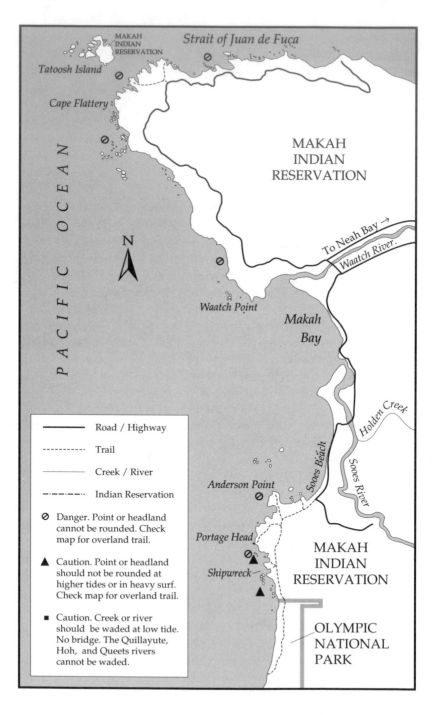

MAKAH
INDIAN
RESERVATION

Strait of Juan de Fuca

Tatoosh Island

Cape Flattery

PACIFIC OCEAN

N

MAKAH
INDIAN
RESERVATION

To Neah Bay →

Waatch River

Waatch Point

Makah
Bay

Holden Creek

Sooes Beach

Sooes River

Anderson Point

Portage Head

Shipwreck

MAKAH
INDIAN
RESERVATION

OLYMPIC
NATIONAL
PARK

─────── Road / Highway

- - - - - - - Trail

─────── Creek / River

─·──·──·─ Indian Reservation

⊘ Danger. Point or headland
cannot be rounded. Check
map for overland trail.

▲ Caution. Point or headland
should not be rounded at
higher tides or in heavy surf.
Check map for overland trail.

■ Caution. Creek or river
should be waded at low tide.
No bridge. The Quillayute,
Hoh, and Queets rivers
cannot be waded.

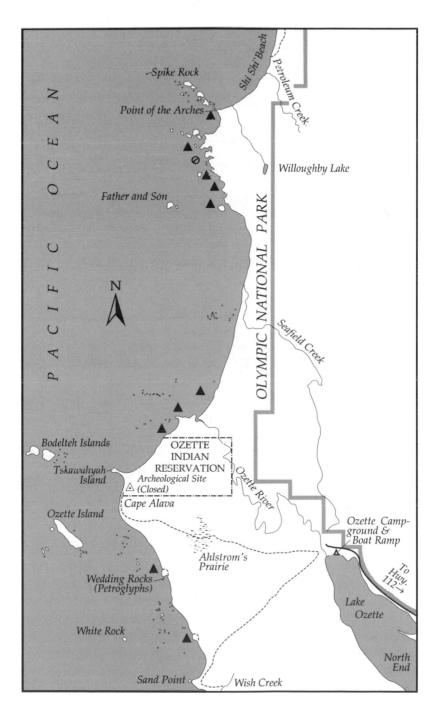

*An unknown woodcarver's
legacy graces this Shi Shi
Beach campsite.*

Olympic National Park boundary). The left fork leads gently down
to Petroleum Creek midway down the beach (no petroleum, great
camping); the right-hand path drops abruptly to the north end of
the beach, with space for perhaps a dozen tents at the bottom, but
no nearby creek.

Shi Shi (pronounced *shy shy*, which is an anglicized version of
the Makah *Sh'ah-sha-ees*, meaning "surf beach") is the Northwest
consensus choice for "Most Beautiful Beach," a 2-mile-long cres-
cent of fine sand with comfortable camping and enough nature
walks to fill a long weekend. An early-morning arrival might find
Shi Shi slowly lifting her gown of silver sea mist, revealing her
rocky guardians and allowing dawn's sunbeams to warm her gentle shores.

Summer-weekend campers should be prepared for company.
It's a 6-hour drive between here and the Puget Sound metropolitan
area, but good weather draws a wide assortment of beach lovers,
ranging from beginning backpackers to wet-suited surfers, even
the occasional nudist.

But, no complaints: it's a miracle that Shi Shi still exists in its natural state. Before the ONP acquired the property in 1976, a small colony of counterculture folk built some rough cabins (since demolished by the rangers) along these shores. Plans for a tourist resort here never quite won the Makahs' blessings.

Take time (at least an hour) to explore north of Shi Shi, crossing from the park into Makah territory. There are no streams and little apparent tent space, but the rocks, sea caves, and tide pools are superb (it's a favorite of intertidal biologists), and at low tide you can walk just under a mile before Portage Head's surf-slickened sidewalls become impassable. Consult the tide table and bring your watch: this is a great place to get trapped by the rising tides.

Rough ridges separate a half-dozen tiny pocket beaches, and the third one up may still have the rusted remains of the only remaining accessible shipwreck on this coast, the World War II–vintage troopship *General M. C. Meigs*. The prow might still be sticking up out of the water just offshore, blending into the surreal sea stacks that imprison it.

*A low tide north of Shi Shi Beach reveals the rusting hulk
of the* General M. C. Meigs.

The *Meigs* was under tow in January 1972 when it broke loose and went up on the rocks here, at what is now known as Shipwreck Cove, spilling 55,000 barrels of fuel oil on the rocks. Damage to the tide-pool denizens was considerable: the local sea urchin and mussel populations declined dramatically, and traces of oil could still be found in the mussels five years later.

Heading south on Shi Shi toward the Point of the Arches, first cross Petroleum Creek (with the aforementioned tent spaces), then a tiny stream issuing from little Willoughby Lake over a mile inland. You can reach the lake via a very hard-to-find, very brushy trail and glimpse it through the trees, but will find the effort required to bushwhack down to it poorly rewarded.

The main attraction here is the mile-long Point of the Arches, a kelp-draped Stonehenge that in profile resembles an abstract map of this coast, all sharp points and deep canyons: a geologic

A natural, wave-carved cavern at Point of the Arches

Wading a shallow spot with Point of the Arches in the background

saw blade. On its northern flank, long washboard ribs of black
rock run seaward like the ribs of a long-buried dinosaur. Low tides
permit inspection of the point's interior tunnels and caves, all lined
with myriad intertidal denizens. In his book *The Sea Runners,*
author Ivan Doig describes the point as "Some mad try here at
walling the Pacific," and indeed these remnants of a prehistoric
headland (some rocks here, much older than their neighbors, were
part of a 144-million-year-old version of the continent) resemble
the ruined temples of a vanished civilization.

Following a lower-than-normal outflowing tide, visitors can
venture near the outermost sea stacks, but should hasten shore-
ward with the rising seas. The waves can return with surprising
speed, and those who tarry on the point may find themselves
swimming for solid ground, a dangerous—and sometimes fatal—
undertaking.

Before Shi Shi became part of the park, hiking south of the
point was a wilderness expedition in every sense; with no trails
and several unroundable points covered with forest nearly too

thick with salal and salmonberry to penetrate. Today, thanks to the trail-building rangers, it's not bad if you're in shape for serious mountain-climbing and carrying a light pack.

Otherwise, get ready for a workout. It's only 2.2 miles from the point to the next long beach, but when you get there, you'll feel as if you've been through the Outward Bound survival school. If the tide is low and you choose to hike around, rather than over, those points with trails, you'll encounter the biggest, baddest boulders this beach boasts. Whether the tide is high or low, you'll have to climb up and down some relatively short but steep mud-and-rock cliffs on the dangling ropes the rangers have thoughtfully provided.

The offshore rocks (notably Father and Son), the sandbox-sized coves (perfect for romantic, no-crowds camping), and the lush forest trails over the unroundable points make this scramble an unforgettable experience. The only drawback is the lack of wa-

Point of the Arches and Shi Shi Beach

ter: at last visit, only one stream—at the second-to-the-southern-most cove—was visible.

Having negotiated the point, southbound hikers can usually amble unhindered for 3.6 miles on the longest open beach on this wilderness coast, with only some cobblestones and perhaps some washed-up kelp-and-seaweed beds to slow the pace. The first tent spaces appear at about 1.5 miles at Seafield Creek, just below eight vacation cabins owned by people who established property rights before the park boundaries were set. Happily, only one house is visible from the beach and the inhabitants are either quiet or else-where; one beach dweller records wildlife activity for the park.

Only the highest tides and waves will close down the small point located about 0.5 mile north of the Ozette River. The north bank of the river's mouth offers lovely surroundings and plentiful tent space, but the river can be brackish; suffer the foul taste or lug a water bag.

High tides and storm waves can make wading the Ozette River next to impossible, as can rainstorm runoff from Lake Ozette 3 miles inland, but the water is usually no more than thigh-deep at low tide in fair weather.

Southbound hikers will find tent space (and possibly a small creek) within a mile of the river on the southern shore, within the "Ozette Triangle" area described in the following chapter under "Cape Alava." The Cape Alava trail begins about 2 miles from the river, and extends inland some 3 miles to Lake Ozette.

Neah Bay

This remote, weatherbeaten fishing town (population: about 1,500) was one of the five original Makah whaling villages that once dotted the coast from Cape Flattery to Cape Alava. Half a century ago, the federal government evacuated and consolidated the villages at Neah Bay, ostensibly to better provide such services as schooling for the children. It is not the westernmost municipality in the continental United States, as one might suppose; that honor goes to La Push.

The early European explorers sought to extend their domin-ion to this corner of the New World, and frequently dropped an-chor at Neah Bay. The Spanish built a fort and settlement in 1792, but abandoned it after a few months. An American trading post opened in 1850. In 1852 a brig up from San Francisco introduced the Makah to smallpox, which killed some two-thirds of the tribe. The present reservation was established three years later.

Today, the fishing-based Makah economy—which is plagued by high unemployment—is supplemented by timber sales from the surrounding 28,000-acre reservation and receipts from summer salmon-boat charters. A grocery store, gas station, and several small restaurants and motels serve tourists. The tribe's future plans include a modern marina and upscale restaurant that would serve yachts and cruise ships. The ethnic Makah Days celebration is in late August.

The Makah Cultural and Research Center

The center (on the south side of the highway at the east end of Neah Bay) is worth a trip to Neah Bay all by itself. It's one of Northwest tourism's best-kept secrets, but it draws visitors from around the world.

Inside the spacious, modern building, artifacts uncovered by archaeologists in the early 1970s from the ancient, mudslide-buried Makah village at Cape Alava—together with authentic whaling canoes and a full-size longhouse—send visitors time-traveling back centuries into a civilization untainted by the European explorers. Old whaling songs drift through the darkened inner sanctums; early photographs depict life as it was here before the turn of the century. Startling dioramas pull the visitor into an environment of virtual reality.

This is truly a great museum. Set aside at least an hour to see it. During non-summer months, call ahead at (206) 645-2711; it may be closed Mondays and Tuesdays.

Cape Flattery

At 1,225 feet above the crashing surf, Cape Flattery is about six times higher than any other headland on this coast, and qualifies as one of the smaller local mountains. Although the Makah have inflicted some dreadful clear-cuts on the forested top, the cape boasts one of the coast's most dramatic seafronts, with labyrinth caverns, sheer cliffs, and jaw-dropping ocean views that include the eyesore lighthouse and coast guard station on Tatoosh Island.

The view from this westernmost point in the continental United States may also include migrating gray whales; in season, it

Cape Flattery

is usually the best whale-watching site on the coast, with the big grays often passing almost directly below. A wide variety of seabirds are also always about; bring binoculars.

Half a mile off the cape, Tatoosh Island figures prominently in Makah history, having served both as a summer fishing camp open to all coastal tribes and as an offshore fortress against raiding tribes (as did James Island off La Push). The island is exceptionally rich in intertidal flora and fauna, but is strictly off-limits to the public. According to local history, Cape Flattery itself once briefly became an island when a huge tsunami swept inland from the sea, cutting the promontory off from the mainland. The year of the event is not recorded.

The road west of Neah Bay branches at the bridge leading to the Shi Shi Beach trailhead, and continues west past a defunct Air Force radar station to the cape's trailhead. Short but rough trails twist down to viewpoints above the surf, and somewhere atop the cape a World War II bunker lies enshrouded in overgrowth. The overlooks have no safety fences: watch your footing.

The round trip (over bumpy roads) and a brief visit at cliffside will consume almost 2 hours, but should not be missed.

2.
The Ozette Triangle

CAPE ALAVA, SAND POINT, AND LAKE OZETTE

Lake Ozette Ranger Station to Cape Alava: *3.1 miles*
Lake Ozette Ranger Station to Sand Point: *2.8 miles*
Cape Alava to Sand Point: *3.1 miles*
Total for Ozette Triangle Hike: *9 miles*

Many hikers get their first sniff of Olympic sea breeze at Cape Alava, a low, forested point amply endowed with both Native American history and expansive scenery.

Starting at the Lake Ozette ranger station, hikers can head to the cape and the now-closed Ozette archaeological site, or to Sand Point, both destinations being easy jaunts of about 3 miles. But with ample camping opportunities along the coast, many stretch this 9-mile triangular loop hike over a weekend. Excursions to Cape Alava should include a side trip to the petroglyphs at Wedding Rocks.

Some will find the rough, 3-mile-long cobblestoned shoreline between the two points to be tiring, but the terrain presents no major obstacles. High tides at the small point at Wedding Rocks and another farther south may compel hikers to take the short trails behind the rocks.

Both Cape Alava and Sand Point have spacious walk-in campgrounds, and the coast between the two headlands is dotted with good tent spaces amongst the trees above the shoreline. Check with the Ozette rangers on the prevailing water situation: at last visit, only one tiny trickle could be found along this stretch, just south of Wedding Rocks. If the coast is dry, lug a water bag from the streams at Sand Point or Cape Alava.

Hikers departing from Lake Ozette can also embark on longer overnight walks north via Cape Alava to Shi Shi Beach, or south from Sand Point, usually to Rialto Beach. See the preceding and following chapters for more information on these routes.

To reach Lake Ozette, turn off Highway 112 about 2 miles west of the town of Sekiu. Watch for the sign; the road is on the left when you're westbound. The lake, ranger station, and campground are some 20 miles down the mostly paved road. Do not be immediately dismayed if the "CAMPGROUND FULL" sign is out; consider the lakeside camping information below.

Lake Ozette

Even without the nearby ocean, this 10-mile-long lake (third-largest in the state) would be a popular destination. It's all within

Ancient canoe "dragway" cleared through the rocks by the Ozette Indians

the ONP and is in near-natural condition, with no commercial development and only a few remaining pre-ONP homes scattered around its shores. It was once the center of a Scandinavian pioneer settlement that survived well into the twentieth century.

The lakeside campground at the north end includes twelve spaces with tables and fireplaces (but no RV hookups), potable water, a swimming beach, rest rooms (no showers), and a pay phone. It seems bigger, and late-arriving tenters on warm-weather weekends may find friendly occupants willing to share the larger campsites. The rangers also allow tents (but not fires) in the picnic-ground area adjacent to the parking lot.

Two boat ramps are located just off the road leading to the ranger station; there's another at the campground. Motorboats are permitted on the lake, an issue of continuing debate hereabouts. Motor noise and (the few) loud campers fade rapidly after Labor Day.

Lake Ozette is a paddler's and small-boat sailor's heaven, at least until a storm blows in suddenly from the ocean a mile away, bringing big gusts and waves. Ericson's Bay, on the lake's western shore, has a small boat-in campground; you can also beach less than a mile south of the campground and take an easy 2-mile trail that ends on a nice coastal beach just south of the Sand Point campground. A bit farther south, another slightly longer trail leads from Allen's Bay on the lake out to lovely Kayostla Beach and the Norwegian Memorial. Both trails are often muddy.

Nonboating hikers may be able to hire a local boat owner to take them to these trailheads. Inquire at the ranger station.

Walking to Cape Alava and Sand Point

Check in at the interpretive kiosk behind the ranger station, read the informative displays inside, then cross the footbridge over the Ozette River. The trail branches: the right fork goes to Cape Alava through historic Ahlstrom's Prairie (wildflowers and scarce traces of early pioneer homes), the left to Sand Point. Each is about 3 miles long, easy walking (the leisurely will spend an hour and a half en route), and mostly on boardwalk (slippery when wet).

Cape Alava

Camping here is gracious, but not lonesome, at least not in the summer months. It's an easy walk from Lake Ozette; some

At the mouth of the Ozette River

people jog out to the beach, some carry their coolers, and a surprising number of folks still want to see the long-closed archaeological site.

Otherwise, tent space is usually ample and sheltered by the forest; water is always plentiful. A ranger may be stationed here during the summer months.

At low tide, beachcomb near Tskawahyah Island for the rusted anchor of the *Austria*, shipwrecked in 1887, and look close for the "dragway" through which the Makah whalers and fishermen pulled their cedar canoes. Although the island (also called Indian or Cannonball Island, for the odd round concreted rocks found there) *is* accessible at low tide, non-Indians should stay off. Like all offshore landforms, the island is part of the off-limits national wildlife refuge, and is also a sacred Makah site. At low tide, the tide pools south of the point are lush with intertidal denizens, on which raccoons may be feasting. Bald eagles sometimes pose on the outer rocks.

101

Some members of this coastline's threatened sea otter population may be visible with the aid of binoculars as they frolic in the kelp beds near Ozette Island, which helps shelter the cape from storms. After being commercially hunted to near-extinction, the sea otters were granted federal protection in 1911 and have re-established colonies in Alaska and California. The small colony on this coastline was transplanted from Alaska in 1970, and is thought to be increasing in size.

The sea otters play a role in one of this coast's myriad multi-dimensional ecological relationships: during their absence from this coast, the population of sea urchins, a favorite otter food source, skyrocketed. Mysteriously, the coast's bald eagles also seemed to be less numerous. The urchins eat kelp, and during this period they nearly destroyed the kelp beds. But when the otters returned, they brought the urchin population back to normal levels, and the kelp beds prospered again. The kelp once again began washing up on shore, offering a food source to a variety of crustaceans and insects. These, in turn, attracted different rodents, which in turn attracted bald eagles, and the eagle population has been on a steady increase, now numbering an estimated twenty-five pairs, with perhaps another fifty birds making random visits.

If the campground seems crowded, head north along the beach; the stretch between the Cape Alava and the Ozette River (less than 2 miles) is dotted with secluded one-tent clearings under the trees, and a small, unreliable creek sometimes provides better water than the river.

High tides can easily impede progress at two small but rough points; the southern one can be traversed via the provided rope. The other's forested crown can be bushwhacked without extreme difficulty. The offshore rocks in here are splendid, featuring some good tide pools and a cave that echoes and reverberates the pounding of the surf.

Ozette Village Site at Cape Alava

In January 1970, a beachcombing schoolteacher spied part of a ghostly structure poking up through the muddy hillside above the beach here, just uncovered by the storm-tossed sea. Archaeologists soon arrived (they had been finding scattered artifacts around Cape Alava for several years) and, over the course of the next decade, uncovered several longhouses that five centuries earlier had

A junior backpacker makes tracks for camp.

been part of a thriving Makah village called Ozette.

The archaeological dig (now closed and smoothed over; no traces remain here) lay above the rocky beach just south of the small point that, at low tide, joins the mainland to tiny Tskawahyah Island. Over a dozen 60-foot-long slant-roofed cedar longhouses, each sheltering up to thirty people, faced the sea. The archaeologists unearthed several that apparently had been buried by a sudden mud slide about A.D. 1500, but some artifacts dated back to 1100.

The sea and forest provided ample food (whales were hunted from canoes), leaving inhabitants time to develop a rich and sophisticated culture. The village remained until the early 1920s, when federal agents moved the remaining Makah to Neah Bay, ostensibly so the children could attend school. The village's few surrounding acres, once confiscated by the federal government, were later returned to the Makah and are now designated as the Ozette Indian Reservation.

Today, all that remains is a modest shelter with a plaque that commemorates the five Makah villages that originally dotted the northern coastline, and the tribal ranger's cottage. An explanatory display, one that outlines the village's history and the archaeological efforts, would be a valuable addition.

Experts agree the Ozette site held one of the most important archaeological treasure chests in North America. More than fifty thousand artifacts dating back to the 1400s are now in cold storage on the Makah reservation in Neah Bay; the best are displayed in the tribe's museum there (see "Makah Cultural and Research Center" in the previous chapter).

Sand Point

Sand Point is low (easily roundable at high tide), flat, and forested, with a great whale-watching nob at the tip. An aging emergency shelter rots gracefully near Wish Creek, which in summer resembles a swamp, but one with good water. Expect neighboring tents in summer, but if you want privacy you can usually find it.

The campground here formerly had a reputation for black bears with a taste for backpacking rations, thus the high steel-pipe racks for "bear bags." Bears are no longer a "problem"; most have been killed off by the logging companies because they destroyed a small number of trees by stripping off the bark for food. But, as elsewhere on the coast, food should still be hung high here; raccoons are numerous.

Seals often haul out on the north-side rocks at low tide. The long beach to the south has good tide pools and an easy 2-mile trail leading back to Ericson's Bay on Lake Ozette, offering an alternate access route.

Wedding Rocks

Located 1 mile south of Cape Alava and about 2 miles north of Sand Point, this otherwise inauspicious little rockpile holds deep ceremonial and religious value in the Makah culture; it probably marked the southern boundary of the Ozette village at Cape Alava and thus the northern limits of Quileute territory, of which La Push, some 20 miles to the south, remains the headquarters.

Some one hundred ancient Makah petroglyphs—renderings of fish, whales, and ceremonial face masks—grace the rocks in scattered locations. One is of a tall-masted sailing ship (see photo on page 74). Other petroglyphs can be found on the Lake Ozette trail and near the archaeological site; their locations are not

Centuries-old petroglyphs grace the Wedding Rocks.

marked. Artistic visitors may take rubbings from the petroglyph surfaces, but those inflicting their own work on the rocks are subject to federal penalties, including imprisonment.

The Makah believed that weddings held here enhanced the bride's fertility (a fertility symbol, an oval design with an intersecting line, is frequently repeated), and these rocks allegedly still reek with spiritual serendipity, at least for those so inclined. New Agers call the point a "power area," and conduct something called "vision quests" here; Christian groups also make pilgrimages. If you hear curious murmurings from behind the boulders, expect to find a party of circled hikers, their heads bowed in fervent prayer.

All visions, miracles, and UFO sightings should be promptly reported to the rangers at Lake Ozette.

3.
The Shipwreck Coast
LAKE OZETTE TO RIALTO BEACH

Lake Ozette to Rialto Beach, via Sand Point: *20.1 miles*

*I*f *all its shipwrecks* were commemorated by marking stones, the Olympic Coast would look like a 60-mile-long cemetery: the bones of countless ancient and modern vessels are distributed all along these rocks. There are only two such monuments, standing over the graves of shipwrecked sailors from Norway and Chile, and they both lie along this portion of the coast.

This part of the coast could appropriately be named after William O. Douglas, associate justice of the Supreme Court, who in 1958 mustered seventy other conservationists to hike this route

A ship's boiler on the beach near the Chilean Memorial

in protest against a planned coastal highway. Wilderness won out, the highway is all but forgotten, and some now-unnamed landmark should someday be officially and justifiably dubbed "Douglas Island" or "Douglas Point."

This is the longest point-to-point wilderness hike on the Olympic Coast (plan on 3 or 4 days), but not necessarily the most rugged: if tides are in their favor (a big "if"), hikers can walk all but a few steps of this route at seaside, albeit over bumpy beaches and much rougher points. The four short high-tide trails require some scrambling, but often compensate with stunning seaward scenery.

See the previous chapter for information on how to reach Lake Ozette.

To reach Rialto Beach and the Mora campground, turn off Highway 101 about 2 miles north of Forks, then bear right at the fork (perhaps pausing to replenish supplies at the small store/restaurant/gas station there), taking the Mora–Rialto Beach road. (The road to the left leads to La Push and the Second and Third Beach trailheads, described in the following chapter.)

Backpackers may park overnight at the beachside parking lot, about 13 miles from Highway 101. The Mora Ranger Station and a 95-space campground (with nature trail and amphitheater) are about 2 miles inland. The campsites are thickly forested, with tables, fireplaces, potable water, and rest rooms. The maximum trailer size is 21 feet and there are no RV hookups.

Backpackers departing from Lake Ozette for the hike south to Rialto Beach may wish to first visit Cape Alava and Wedding Rocks before beginning the trek south past Sand Point. This option adds about 3 miles of beach hiking to the trip. Others may wish to travel downlake by boat to either Ericson's Bay or Allen's Bay on the lake's western shore, then hike the overland trails to the coast. These options are described in the previous chapter.

Sand Point is an excellent first-night camp for those arriving late in the day; tent space and water are always plentiful. Otherwise, continue south toward Yellow Banks over the lovely 2-mile-long beach, passing the trailhead leading east to Ericson's Bay on Lake Ozette and some nice tide pools at the south end.

The series of small points just north of the Yellow Banks beach are easy to round with a low tide; a natural rock tunnel usually allows passage at higher tides.

Yellow Banks, named after the high clay cliffs above the

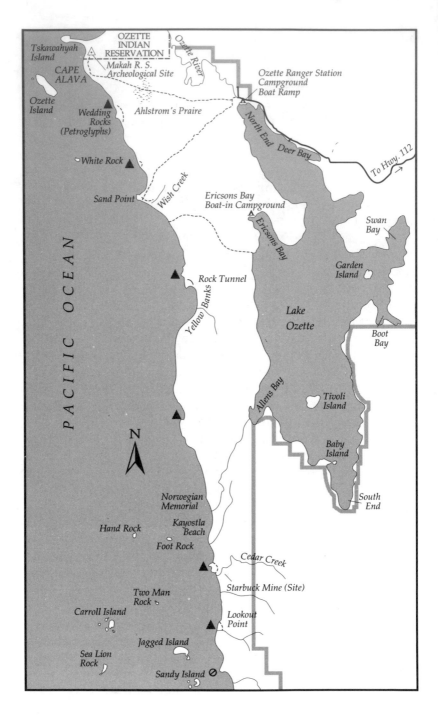

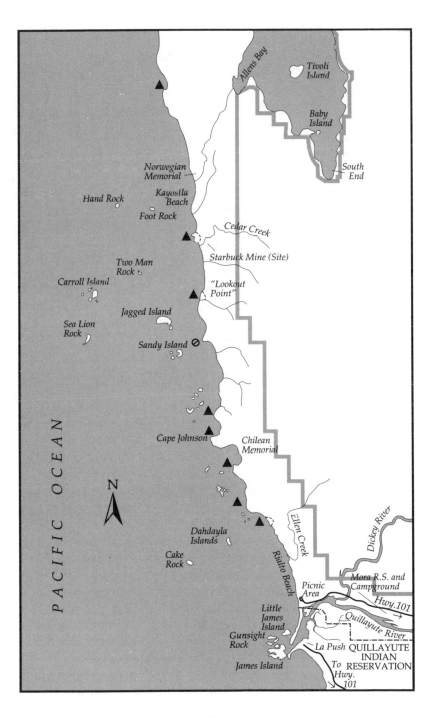

beach, has very limited tent space, several small creeks, and a huge fine-sand beach that is very flat and vulnerable to high-tide waves in stormy weather. The beach is completely open to the sea, with no islands or sea stacks to break the waves. Digging for butter clams is possible in season; check with the rangers.

As you continue southbound, now some 5 miles from Lake Ozette, you next traverse about 2.5 miles of unobstructed coast-line—a rough beach intersected by a half-dozen creeks and a few possible tent spaces—to the next tide-affected point, about 8 miles from Lake Ozette. The small point has no high-tide trail over the top, but offers a northside waiting area with comfortable drift-log perches, a fairly easy rounding, and a picturesque rock arch at the tip.

After another 2 miles of cobblestones, you will reach Kayostla Beach. Like Yellow Banks, it is broad and open, but less exposed to high waves; the view includes a tide-pool–filled reef, with Foot Rock and Hand Rock well out to sea. Forest trails lead to a peaceful grove occupied by the Norwegian Memorial (the history of this and the Chilean Memorial are described in "Footprints in the Sand") and eastward to Allen's Bay on Lake Ozette. An emergency shelter stands beside the reliable creek, and tent space is plentiful.

Now more than 11 miles from Lake Ozette, climb a sand ladder up a short but steep high-tide trail over a small headland at the south end of Kayostla Beach, or walk the point. On the south side are some tent spaces beside Cedar Creek, where the rangers some-times have a summer station. Just south is the long-defunct Star-buch Mine site, with some rusted mining equipment shrouded in salmonberry. Visitors are welcome to pan for any gold that Mr. Starbuch might have missed.

As you walk south on this beach toward the next point, a mile distant, a pretty covey of islands comes into view: Two Man Rock, Carroll, Jagged, and Sea Lion Rock. In the summer of 1992, a biologist spotted a Steller's sea lion pup with its mother on Carroll Island, an event that led to speculation that this threatened species may be resuming breeding here, an activity not seen since early white settlers hunted them to near-extinction. Even if the tide's low, the summit of the next (unnamed) headland deserves a visit, and not just for the tremendous view. Climb the sand-ladder and peek into the rustic abandoned shack at cliff's edge, once an out-

A rainy afternoon on Rialto Beach

post in the World War II Coast Lookout System. In the absence of
official nomenclature, we'll call it "Lookout Point."

Today, along with a pair of overgrown concrete bunkers atop
Portage Head, this shack is the only remaining vestige of the hardy
but untested band of soldiers, local militia and their dogs, who
were America's first line of defense against enemy invasion or
ship-to-shore communication in the war's early days. There's tent
space near the cabin, as well as near the creek on the headland's
south flank.

Now at a bit more than 12 miles from Lake Ozette, traverse
another mile of fine-sand beach, one with several creeks but no
promising tent spaces. High tides or storms could block this
stretch. At the beach's south end is the only always-unroundable

111

headland on this stretch of coast, but it's a little one and its low spine is easy to scramble.

High water could easily be a problem on the following 1.4-mile stretch of beach as well: at last visit, downed trees protruded horizontally seaward, forming an interesting obstacle course. Otherwise this is a pretty beach, one with several possible tent spaces, several creeks (one of them a unique low waterfall), and a family of shy river otters.

Next, at about 15 miles from Lake Ozette, is the point north of Cape Johnson and some rugged rock-hopping. A nice beach (with several tent spaces but no creek) intervenes; then comes the cape, an even-longer stretch of rugged rock-hopping. Medium-high tides close both these points, and there's no trail over.

If fatigue prevails after the traverse of Cape Johnson and its sister point to the north, a camp beside the Chilean Memorial (16.4 miles from Lake Ozette) may well be in order. If so, it may be a memorable evening: this is a beautiful but eerie little cove. Wildlife seems strangely absent, perhaps because of the lack of a creek, although trickles may be found back in the woods, and the tide pools are fecund.

Just offshore, flat-topped Cake Rock, jagged Dahdayla Island, and the bay's own guardian sea stacks have shredded more than their share of ships (some evidence of which may still rest at shoreside). Two of them, both Chilean vessels, are commemorated by the small monument (described in "Footprints in the Sand"), with victims buried beneath. There is something out of the ordinary here: with clouds sailing past a full moon and with a driftwood fire flickering, even those who scoff at the supernatural may glimpse strange shadows and hear Spanish whispers on the sea breeze. Bring a friend.

Some 3.6 miles now distance you from the Rialto Beach parking lot, about half of it over rough rock. Wait for a low or outgoing tide, first at the point at the south end of the Chilean Memorial cove (not mentioned on the maps), then along the north face of a steep-faced headland more than a mile south of the memorial. Watch for rough trails in the higher rocks, but there are no alternative overland trails. Between the two are several creeks and possible tent spaces.

Good tide pools grace the coastline north of Hole-in-the-Wall, an imposing black monolith bored through by the waves, and some tent space is evident. A huge slab of grooved, flat sandstone forms a natural deck for whale and wave watching, and, according to reports, whales come quite close to the rocky point to the north of Hole-in-the-Wall. Fishing is reported to be good from the outer rocks.

Hole-in-the-Wall's tunnel can be traversed at lower tides, although the wet rocks underfoot, apparently smoothed by heavy foot traffic, are exceptionally slick. A steep trail behind the rock allows high-tide passage.

With its easy access, 1.5-mile-long Rialto Beach is a popular destination; you'll likely see dozens of strollers, even on a wet and windy winter afternoon. Rock climbers may be practicing on a tall shoreside sea stack. Tent space is plentiful north of Ellen Creek (rare ospreys may still have a nest in the nearby trees); camping is forbidden south of it. At low tide some tide pools appear, and the mile-long sand spit just south of the parking area provides close-up looks at big, cliff-sided James Island and its attendant family of sea stacks.

Digging for clams on the beach at Yellow Banks

4.
The Wildcatter Coast

THIRD BEACH TO OIL CITY

Third Beach Trailhead on the La Push Road
to Oil City: *17.1 miles*

The above title, "The Wildcatter Coast," is a tongue-in-cheek salute to the petroleum industry, which limited its onshore, pre-park search for oil to this rugged section of coastline. Little evidence of their explorations remains, the industry having turned its attentions to the offshore regions, and the natural terrain is in pristine condition.

Pristine, certainly, and rugged. This trek features the coast's most challenging stream crossing (Goodman Creek), as well as one of its trickiest stretches of surfside rocks (the little patch just south of Mosquito Creek). The hike will probably consume 3 days from start to finish, with an R&R day at Toleak Point heartily recommended.

The La Push Road departs from U.S. 101 and heads west to the ocean at a point about 2 miles north of Forks, a logging town with tourist facilities.

The road splits at about 8 miles; stay to the left, or pause at the store/restaurant/gas station for supplies. (The north or right-hand fork leads to the ONP's Mora Ranger Station and campground and to Rialto Beach, described in the previous chapter.)

The parking area for the Third Beach trail is on the south side of the road about 3 miles after the fork and about 11 miles from the U.S. 101–La Push Road junction.

Farther west lie the seaside fishing village of La Push and First Beach (which is within the small Quileute Indian Reservation but is open to the public), and the roadside trailhead parking lot for Second Beach, which is (like Third Beach) included within the ONP.

After leaving the roadside parking lot on La Push Road behind and passing a privy and backpacking-registration kiosk,

A flock of seabirds feasts on fish.

begin the gentle 1.5-mile forest trail to Third Beach. The silent forest gradually fills with the sound of surf as the trail drops steeply to tent spaces above the beachside mouth of a stream. A logjam of driftwood timber lines the beach's upper rim at trail's end; the less agile may find it too difficult to negotiate, but, if so, the view of Strawberry Bay from here is just fine.

Third Beach is also the turnaround point for many less ambitious hikers: it's a nice, quick, out-to-the-beach-and-back day-hike, but one with ample space for tents both on the beach and back in the trees, and a selection of babbling brooks.

North of trail's end, a receding tide permits inspection of the slippery tide pools lining the south flank of Teahwhit Head, but not passage around and under the bluff. There's no trail over, and Second Beach must be reached through some ferocious bushwhacking or, preferably, a return to the road. The thick forest above the north end of the beach conceals some rusted oil-drilling equipment the wildcatters abandoned back at the turn of the century, the first in an ongoing series of (so far unsuccessful) attempts to rezone the coast for heavy industry.

Starting south, cruising on a fine-sand carpet, pass more creeks and tent space, as well as an onshore mini–sea stack with a lone brave spruce clinging to its summit, and approach a high unnamed waterfall tumbling over a cliff on the north flank of Taylor

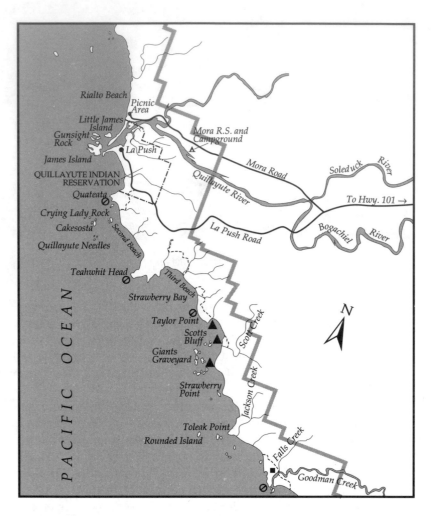

Point at the far south end of the beach (the sea eroded the bank faster than the creek could cut down through it). The marked trail over Taylor Point begins well before the end of the beach; with time and a low tide, the rocks at the south end can be partially explored, but not rounded.

First, before starting over Taylor Point, take a long look at the sand ladders gracing the headland's northern flank. Although the ascent is reasonably safe, the less agile may wisely opt to turn around here, and climbers should keep an eye and ear tuned to rocks falling from the bare cliffs above. Having negotiated these

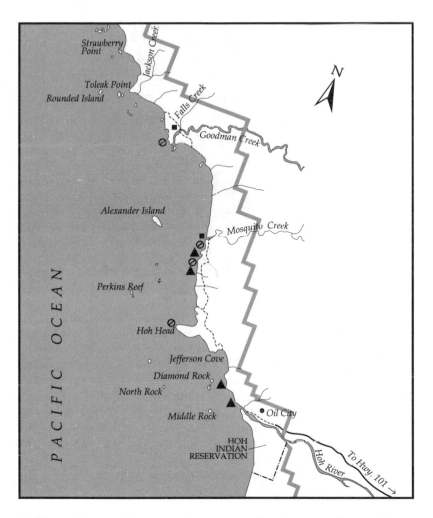

ladders (four, at last count), prepare for more on the southern flank.

The rugged 1.2-mile forest trail in-between crosses a log-bridged creek (which feeds the Third Beach waterfall) but offers few views seaward.

Note: Check the tide table before beginning the climb over Taylor Point; some rocks on the point's southern flank may be impassable at high tide. If so, take a break or, if nightfall is imminent, retreat to trailside tent spaces atop the headland.

After descending from Taylor Point, you are 3 miles from the

*Rock-dancing
with a rising tide*

roadside trailhead (and about 14 miles from Oil City). It seems much farther; casual tourists have long since turned back and the rhythms of the sea begin to pervade the senses. A pretty 0.5-mile-long beach with a few trickles (but no obvious campsites) leads to a pile of rocks at the base of Scott's Bluff (Mr. H. Scott was the first of several pioneers to homestead here in the late 1890s; no traces remain), where even a medium tide can send walkers up the short, steep trail over the bluff. A close-in sea stack shows the bluff was once a protruding headland. A shelter and nice campsites can be found on the south side of the bluff; cobblestoned Scott Creek may require boots-off wading.

Now 4 miles from the road, approach the tombstonelike Giants' Graveyard—a family of about a dozen sea stacks, resting place of countless shipwrecked mariners. The grim record begins with a Spanish frigate lost in the late 1700s; no wreckage of any remains. High tides will block passage around the small point just east of the Graveyard, but Strawberry Point, the next protuberance south, shuts down only at high tide in storm season: both have rough routes along the upper rims. The beaches between are mostly rocky walking. Strawberry Point's big flat-topped guardian bird sanctuary and thus off-limits to humans.

There are several small creeks between Scott's Bluff and Toleak Point, but no comfortable tent sites, even though the beach smoothes out. No matter.

Toleak Point (6.4 miles from the La Push Road; about 11 miles from Oil City) is the place to drop anchor for at least a night. Sheltered by a covey of spire-domed islands (notably mile-out Rounded Island, once Toleak's tip), the point served as an ancient Quileute fishing camp, and the tribal elders sometimes still bring the kids here in canoes to study the old ways. Two longhouses stood here until the early 1900s, and, with some archaeological sleuthing, you can find the old Quileute middens, small garbage dumps full of shells. The point also served as an outpost for the coastal home guard during World War II.

Space for tents is plentiful but never crowded, and several creeks trickle seaward. A ranger is sometimes stationed here in the summer, there's a rotting potty up in the trees, great tide pools are located off the point, and a family of bald eagles might swoop over your camp to check you out. Seals are usually around, possibly a few sea lions as well. In season, scramble up the rocks on the point to whale-watch.

Toleak reeks of serendipity. Rest and allow yourself to be lulled by its idyllic ambience, then continue south on a soft, mile-long beach (tent space and creeks down here too) to a confrontation with the Goodman Creek–Falls Creek headland, unroundable at water's edge. A 1.5-mile trail rises sharply from the beach and tours through beautiful forest, interrupted first by Falls Creek and its photogenic waterfall. At last visit, a log bridged the creek, but it is otherwise wadable. With an outgoing low tide, the adventurous can follow this creek to its juncture with Goodman Creek, the rocky bank of which may then be scrambled almost all the way to the ocean.

The path soon stops at Goodman Creek, best considered a small river. Indians and early settlers used its banks as a link between the coast and the inland Bogachiel Valley, a route still visible in places, as are high stumps pocked with notches in which pioneer loggers anchored the springboards that served as sawing platforms.

Goodman Creek is usually slow and shallow enough to permit careful wading by average hikers, but a high tide below or heavy runoff from upstream can easily boost the water level to the danger point. A helpful log may still partially bridge the current. If the creek looks too fast and deep and the tide is coming in, consider waiting for the ebb; there's some nice tent space on the north side and possible places on the south.

After descending a sand ladder on the headland's south side, those with time and tides on their side can detour north along the beach, first rounding a low point, and see the rocky spillway where the creek has carved its path to the ocean. Such junctures of fresh and salt waters are biologically rich, and are always active meeting places for a variety of birds and sea creatures; sea otters are frequently seen in the neighborhood.

Now almost 10 miles from the road, resume cruising speed on smooth sand. A close-in (but off-limits) sea stack presents itself for inspection at low tide; tent space is evident and a few trickles cross the beach a bit farther south.

Flat-topped Alexander Island, long and low, now rises a mile offshore on the southern horizon, serving as headquarters for the state's largest population of Cassin's auklets (an estimated 55,000), a rarely seen, sea-feeding bird that flies and eats at night to escape the gulls, its fiercest predator.

Due east of the island, Mosquito Creek slithers out of the forest and across a broad, soft beach to meet the ocean. The name may discourage tourism, but no skeeters are evident and the camping is gracious and open to the ocean. Ample tent space is available on both sides of the creek, which is usually easily wadable at low tide. There's a log shelter on the south bank near the trail that leads south along the bluffs above the ocean.

Here, about 11 miles from the La Push Road and some 6 miles from Oil City, the walking gets a bit more strenuous. The choice is between a rough 3.5-mile trail through the forest above the ocean, one with only occasional views, or a short but potentially dangerous scramble over a series of big, wet rocks beginning about 0.5-mile south of the creek, followed by a smooth beach often washed by the winter storm tides.

Let the weather and tide table make the decision: if the tide and waves are low, cautious hikers may enjoy the rocky route at surf's edge, but should even then be prepared for some careful wading. Short trails detour behind the biggest rocks, and finding the mouth of the pretty, wave-carved cavern that hides in these

Sand ladders should be ascended by only one climber at a time.

barnacled, kelp-draped canyons should help compensate for any scrapes or soggy shorts. Just don't take a chance on getting caught in here by the incoming tide.

After these rocks, those who take the waterfront tour have an easy mile-long beach walk (with a creek and some possible tent space) before climbing a short but very steep trail up the bank, one that merges with the overland route. A pretty cavern near the trail's bottom could serve as shelter from a storm. Northbound walkers, after mulling the tide table, may slide down here to reach the beach route to Mosquito Creek.

Southbound beachwalkers can, by continuing on past this trail at low tide, explore Secret Cove below Hoh Head's northern cliffs. At Jefferson Cove, on the head's southern side via the forest trail, a low tide will allow exploration of Boulder Beach, where big round stones have fallen from the cliffs above. Amateur geologists will note that the soft *melange* rock on the head's flanks is wearing thin and will eventually erode completely, turning the hard sandstone core into an offshore landform and necessitating a name change to Hoh Island. Whale-watching season is a good time to bushwhack out to the head's tip, a side trip that should be undertaken within the next millennium.

Having reached Jefferson Cove, some 14 miles from this beachwalk's beginning, less than 3 miles separate you from the Oil City trailhead. Two small points may be impassible at high tides; no trails lead over, but otherwise the rocky beach is walkable at all tide levels. There's tree-sheltered space for tents above the beach just north of the Hoh River's mouth; reliable creeks are nearby.

The trail along the river's north bank to the Oil City parking area occasionally washes out, necessitating a scramble along the rocky riverbank or a bushwhack through the trees above, depending on tides and river levels.

Oil City

This is the ONP's least-used official coastal access point, but it gets you out into the scenery just as fast as the others and offers decent camping on the beach less than a mile from the car. It's the site of a long-gone oil-boom camptown (see "Footprints in the Sand" for Oil City's history), and is used more by fishing enthusiasts than by backpackers.

Finding a high-tide route through ragged rock

The Oil City Road leads oceanward from U.S. 101 about 0.5 mile north of the Hoh River bridge. Cottonwood State Park, on the river about 2 miles down the road, has 6 campsites, a maximum trailer length of 21 feet, toilets, and potable water. Camp here if darkness threatens to fall before you can start the sometimes-washed-out trail along the river to the beach. Rustic farms grace the 10 miles of gravel leading to Oil City and the road's terminus; herds of large, gentle bovines stand in the middle of it.

Backpackers should sign in at the kiosk at the Oil City turnaround, then head for the beach through a wildflower-strewn tunnel of overhanging cottonwood and alder, noting floats for the Hoh tribe's salmon nets in the river. Their small reservation includes the river's southern shore.

La Push and First Beach

The fishing village of La Push is on the ocean at the end of the south (left) fork of the La Push Road, 13.5 miles from that road's junction with U.S. 101 and about 5 miles from the fork. First Beach, which lies adjacent to the town, is easily reachable from the parking area just east of the village.

French explorers are thought to have named this place *La Bouche* (the mouth) for its location at the Quillayute River's opening, but it served as the ancient home of the Quileute Indians for thousands of years before European-Americans began arriving in the mid-nineteenth century.

Because the river mouth offered a small harbor (now protected by man-made breakwaters) it became the first white settlement on this northern coastline and the only port facility ever, one employed today by the coast guard station and a dozen tribal salmon-fishing boats. Seagoing kayakers also put in here.

The Quileute, surrounded by the ONP coastal park, continue to protest today about the cramped boundaries enforced on them by treaties signed in the mid- and late-1890s. The tribe's growing population (now some 574 members) presses the limits of their allotted 925 acres, but their unique language—apparently unrelated to any other in the world—is now spoken by only three elderly members.

La Push's commercial district (it's the westernmost town in the Lower Forty-eight) offers all the usual amenities to tourists, mostly visitors who come to fish the rivers and ocean. Native handicrafts are sold at several locations and traditional cedar dug-out whaling canoes are on display. Some rooms and cabins offer spectacular First Beach views; lodging is best reserved well in advance. The private campground and the trailer/RV park (with hookups) seem to have abundant space.

First Beach is easily accessible from the town and is scenic, due to the close-in islands, notably big, steep-sided James, the tribe's traditional stronghold against Makah raids. First Beach is fine for a picnic and beachcombing, but camping isn't allowed.

Second Beach

The trail to Second Beach begins just east of La Push on the south side of the road, about 13 miles from U.S. 101 and less than a mile (easy roadside walking distance) from La Push. It is a separate destination, and is not connected by trail to either La Push and First Beach or to Third Beach. The gentle trail is less than a mile long.

This is a classic North Coast seascape in a small package: a romantic swath of fine sand guarded by close-in sea stacks, with tide pools and even a little optional rock scrambling waiting at both ends of the 1.5-mile-long beach.

You can see it all in a few hours, but overnight camping here is delightful, particularly in storm-watching season when the tourists thin out. If not for the La Push foghorn's low moan, you'd think you were miles from civilization. Three small creeks cross the sand. Space for several tents lies under the trees at the north end of the beach; there's more toward the south end, farther away from the trail, but it's on the beach and could be exposed to higher tides.

The offshore geology features the unique, sharp-tipped, 85-foot-high Quillayute Needle (a name also given to the family of sea stacks around the Needle, as well as the section of the rock-island wildlife refuge lying offshore). At the beach end of the access trail lies a rare, two-story-high volcanic rock, scraped off the ocean floor by the subduction process described in "A Mountain from the Sea." Experienced rock climbers may attempt its summit.

Two magnificent headlands bracket Second Beach like book-ends: Quateata on the north, Teahwhit Head on the south, each offering tide pools on their Second Beach flanks. Low tides will allow careful wading some distance out, but not passage around.

Sunset after a storm on Second Beach

Quateata has an arch near its tip where big waves slosh through, and the intrepid can venture out along its ridge to watch the massive waves arrive.

A good low tide will permit access to the knife-edged, upreaching finger rocks at the tip of Teahwhit, where the Russian freighter *Lamut* was washed up and trapped in a storm in 1943. High seas prevented rescue by boat, so coast guardsmen bushwhacked out to the point, tied their bootlaces together, and, while perched on a knife-edged cleaver, lowered this fragile line to the Russian sailors clinging to the listing deck of their sinking ship in the churning chaos below. The Russians tied a rope to the shoelaces, the coast guardsman pulled up the rope and the shivering sailors shinnied up the sheer cliff to safety. Fifty-three were saved; one drowned.

Perhaps someday trails over these promontories (both are unroundable at water's edge) will link Third, Second, and First beaches, permitting an uninterrupted hike from the Hoh River to the Quillayute River.

5.
Destruction Island

HOH RIVER TO QUEETS RIVER

Hoh River to Queets River: *14.7 miles*

This is a gentle shoreline, at least in comparison to the coast to the north. It is unbroken by major headlands, points, or sea stacks; the highway on its upper rim runs nearly straight. But it is fully exposed to the pounding Pacific, and only omnipresent Destruction Island, always looming on the near horizon, breaks the ocean's vast expanse.

If this southernmost section of park coast lacks the scenic drama and geologic chaos of the unpaved, true-wilderness coast to the north, it is also much easier walking. This stretch of coastline is popular with nonhiking tourists, contemplative strollers, and kids too young for long walks.

The parking areas (all with toilets and quick-info nature signs) are all only a few minutes' walk from beachside. Some visitors might find the trails down to the beaches a mite steep, but they're otherwise wide and smooth.

Walks of any length should begin with a check on the next high tide; storm waves can make beachwalking difficult or potentially dangerous at any tide level. Tide tables are posted at the Kalaloch Ranger Station (located just south of the tourist village on the inland side), and at the inn.

Beach camping is forbidden on this section, but picnicking is permitted, and many choice spots will present themselves. Most people find the water far too cold for swimming, even when the seas are calm and skies are sunny. Waders should always watch for unexpected waves and drift logs in the surf.

The most scenic stop on this stretch of coastline is Ruby Beach, located at the north end where the highway turns back inland. Its sands are laced with traces of reddish garnet (as they are elsewhere), thus the name. Offshore lie some tourist-trampled tide pools.

Tides and waves permitting, northbound hikers can usually

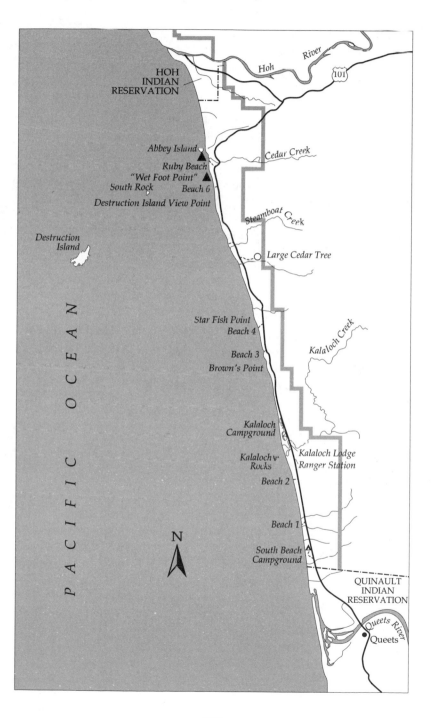

HOH
INDIAN
RESERVATION

Hoh *River*

101

Cedar Creek

Abbey Island
Ruby Beach
"Wet Foot Point"
South Rock *Beach 6*
Destruction Island View Point

Steamboat Creek

Destruction
Island

Large Cedar Tree

Star Fish Point
Beach 4

Kalaloch Creek

Beach 3
Brown's Point

Kalaloch
Campground

Kalaloch Lodge
Ranger Station

Kalaloch
Rocks

Beach 2

N

Beach 1

South Beach
Campground

QUINAULT
INDIAN
RESERVATION

Queets River
Queets

P A C I F I C   O C E A N

rock-hop Cedar Creek easily, round a small point in the lee of Abbey Island, a mammoth chunk of Pleistocene-era volcanic rock named by a pioneer who thought it resembled a cathedral, and walk below 150-foot-high cliffs toward the Hoh Indian Reservation and the mouth of the Hoh River, some 3 miles distant. The reservation is small and has no tourist facilities.

The Hoh, who are related to the Quileute Indians at La Push, may have salmon nets in the river (this is one of the few good salmon rivers remaining on the peninsula), and local fisherfolk may be found casting into the surf anywhere along this section of coast. The coastline north of the Hoh River is reached via Oil City.

Those heading south from Ruby Beach will need a fairly low tide to round a low point (known locally and appropriately as Wet Foot Point) a mile down, and may then begin looking for the scarce remains of an old shipwreck in the vicinity of Beach Trail 6. The access trails on this section of coastline are numbered consecutively from south to north; Beach Trail 5 has been removed from service.

In another mile, the cliffs under the Destruction Island roadside viewpoint (a popular vista for whale watching, in season) loom above another tide-affected point. The steep trail up to the highway is risky and lacks official sanction.

Destruction Island

This sixty-acre table-topped rock, more than three miles offshore, does not receive visitors, due to its status as one of the Olympic Coast's most important seabird refuges. The lighthouse is no longer in service.

Some 6,000 years ago, Destruction Island was the coastline's western edge; since then, the sea has moved the coast back at the rate of about three hundred feet every one hundred years. The island is protected by its westward reefs of deep sandstone, but big storm waves still blow over it.

With no other true islands between here and San Francisco, Destruction Island served as a landmark and an anchorage for the early explorers, but many ships have wrecked on its sharp reefs.

In the next 3.5 miles, as you head south, pass two unnumbered trails that lead up to the highway, and four small creeks. At Star Fish Point, just north of Beach Trail 4, the bare sandstone rocks reveal layers in the rock, called strata, that were tipped at angles by

Mysterious Destruction Island lies 3 miles offshore.

movements in the earth's crust, beginning about forty million years ago.

Sharply angled strata appear again around Brown's Point, more than 0.5 mile farther south, where high tides may again bring progress to a halt both north and south of the point. Look for a small arch bored through the rock by the waves. Beach Trail 3, just north of Brown's Point, offers close-up views of the rigors visited upon the seaside spruce and alder by the salt spray from the ocean, and the local tide pools reveal the damage wrought by excessive human visitation. But, all in all, this area is perhaps the prettiest stop south of Ruby Beach.

The shoreline is then easy walking for the 2.5 miles south to the Kalaloch tourist village.

Kalaloch

Once the site of a turn-of-the-century fish cannery, Kalaloch (*clay-lock*) today offers a complete array of tourism facilities, but reservations at the lodge and ocean-view cabins should be made well in advance. The gas station's store is well stocked, and the inn and restaurant have an excellent reputation.

The dainty gazebo at cliffside is handy for foul-weather

Ruby Beach and Abbey Island

whale watching, and a staircase links the lodge with a pretty beach complete with creek and a set of wave-washed rocks. The beach to the north sometimes yields razor clams, but check at the ranger station before digging.

The park's secluded campground north of the lodge has 179 spaces (with tables and fireplaces), allows trailers 21 feet and under (no hookups), and provides flush toilets, a dump station, and telephone. A short nature trail tours the nearby old-growth forest. Nesting RVs often block the view of the ocean.

South of Kalaloch, the beach narrows and becomes much rockier, but can usually be traversed at high tide. Beach trails 1 and 2 link the shoreline to highwayside parking, and are lined with Sitka spruce sprouting large, odd bulbous tumors (apparently benign) called burls. Another specimen—the world's largest western red cedar—surveys the coast from its home on the inland side of the highway just south of the Destruction Island viewpoint.

Backpackers should not be misled by the "primitive" label given the South Beach Campground, just north of the park's southern boundary and 3 miles south of Kalaloch. While it provides a lavatory, it has no potable water or comfortable tent spaces, and during warm-weather months a large flock of RVs appears to be in continuous residence. It's closed in winter.

Southbound hikers can cross the park boundary, enter the Quinault Indian Reservation, and traverse a widening but still-rocky beach 0.5 mile to the mouth of the Queets River. The Quinaults' headquarters town of Queets is on Highway 101 a mile upriver, on the southern bank.

Epilogue: Walking with the Whales

Mystery dances on the Easter Island sea stacks, in the smugglers' fogbanks, in the holy-water tide pools where shells and stones arrange themselves in lines of transcendental *haiku*. Mystery dances on the coast, in the deep quiet of her sea-green forests and in the howl of her shipwreck storms.

I like to imagine that Herman Melville was out looking for whales at Point of the Arches when he wrote: "There is, one knows not what sweet mystery about this sea, whose gently awful stirrings seem to speak of some hidden soul beneath." When an anemone greets you with a wink, when a rare sea otter bobs to the surface and returns your smile, you feel the mystery for an instant and you sense that nature knows you're there.

"Always," wrote Rachel Carson, "the edge of the sea remains an elusive and indefinable boundary." Yet the clues keep teasing us: ocean covers seven-tenths of the earth, and seven-tenths of our bodies—the bodies of all living creatures—are salty water containing the same chemicals as the sea. It is generally accepted scientific theory that all earthly life began at seaside, appeared from protoplasmic vapors zapped awake by primal lightning. Perhaps the planet reaches a sort of critical mass at the seam of earth and sea, and living things feel it. Perhaps we are pilgrims to the motherland. The mystery slips through our fingers like an ebbing tide. This coast has, as Barry Lopez noted of the Arctic, "an identity of its own, still deeper and more subtle than we can know."

This sense of nature's powerful mystery can easily convince us that these rocks, this sea, these birds and fishes, are permanent, untouchable. "This," we sigh, contentedly watching a lipstick sunset fading behind shadowed sea stacks, a calm sea tickling our toes, "is the way it has always been." But in the time since the last glaciers melted away twelve thousand years ago (a tiny fraction of a tick on the cosmic clock), these rocks and beaches have been somewhat altered, and the first human residents would scarcely know the place today.

And the coast has changed drastically in the last century or so. Bordering the sea is a forest that *looks* like it's been there forever, but most of it has grown up since it was logged off at the turn of the century. It is not a synthetic tree farm, but it's not quite nature; not for a few more centuries, anyway. There used to be bears on these beaches, and now, partly because the bears are nearly gone, the deer are tame as poodles. Sea lions and sea otters have all but vanished. Salmon used to crowd the rivers, and there used to be an eagle on just about every other snag. There once were people here who could live on what they found in the sea and forest. All that was real nature. All that has changed.

You know the feeling in your stomach when you pick the paper up off your doorstep and read a headline that says, "oil spill." It's the same feeling you get when you're waiting for a kid or a spouse to get home, the phone rings, and a strange voice says, "police" and "accident." Something dies inside, and you're never again quite the same person. On some coast, somewhere, things are dying by the thousands: plants, animals, birds. Nature.

Nature is dying on the Olympic Coast every day, suffocating in little patches of waste oil and chemicals dumped from those ships we see chugging across the horizon. You don't hear about this on the news. The media don't show up until these vessels meet with catastrophic accident, as (most recently) the fish processor *Tenyo Maru* did in July 1991. It carried hundreds of thousands of gallons of engine oil, as most large ocean vessels do. When their holds are ruptured, their oil is almost always swept landward by the waves. Then a lot of nature dies. The TV news shows the oily

A spectacular sunset lights a pacific sea.

seabirds flopping around, interviews a few enraged environmentalists, and then cuts to a car commercial.

Right now, the Northwest environmental news is focused on logging. When you fly into Seattle on a clear day, you see that the surrounding mountains look like a bumpy lawn that's been mowed with a dull blade. Like the forests, the resident wildlife is managed, with emphasis on man. Wolves and grizzlies are no longer at the top of nature's food chain; the few that remain venture out of the national parks and wilderness refuges at their own risk. Because of logging and too much fishing, the wild salmon runs are all but gone. We are left with what the scientists call "biological islands," and the smaller the islands get, the faster the wildlife dies away.

The mountains of the Olympic National Park look like an island from the air, the primal forest surrounded by the clear-cuts. The coastal strip is another island, with the tree farms and reforestation failures at its back, but with a real and still-fertile ocean pounding the shore. Oil and depletion of the fisheries are the ocean's clear-cuts.

The offshore oil-drilling issue comes and goes around here; at this writing, it's all but forgotten, but it could come back very rapidly. If the petroleum industry is eventually allowed to drill for oil and gas offshore, the Olympic coast will change a lot, and for a very long time. Maybe—probably—forever. Whether offshore oil is permitted here depends partly on how much pressure the oil industry wants to put on the government. As I write this with the 1992 presidential election underway, the Bush administration prefers petroleum to petrels.

There isn't much oil and gas out there—about enough to fuel the country for half a week, maybe only a day or so—but it might take the oil industry thirty-five years, half a human lifespan, to get what they want of it. During that time, the brightly lit, ten-story-high platforms would each disgorge hundreds of thousands of tons of toxic "drilling muds" and millions of barrels of oily "production water" into the sea. When the breeze is landward, as it usually is, the air would have a chemical odor, and tarballs would litter the beach, as they do near offshore rigs in Southern California. That is a fair description of your average Third World industrial park.

That's if everything went smoothly. Nobody is sure how

many platforms would be out there, but the largest oil spill ever came from a single offshore oil rig in the Gulf of Mexico. If a rig ruptured on these rough seas, control would be impossible, even if containment crews were ready. Clean-up would be near-futile: only eight percent of Exxon's oil was recovered from the more-protected Prince William Sound. Biologists say that a large breeding-season oil spill, whether from an offshore-oil platform or a foundering tanker, could cause virtually permanent destruction of the coast's seabird and sea otter populations.

Few Northwesterners favor offshore oil, even those on the economically depressed Peninsula: the oil rigs would dampen tourism, employ very few local workers, and would contribute little tax revenue. Therefore, so far, even our most conservative politicians have opposed offshore drilling. But beyond the state-owned five-mile limit, the waters are federal. The next congressional oil battle will be over the Arctic National Wildlife Refuge, which may yield a few month's worth of fuel. After that will come the battle for the Olympic Coast.

In 1988, Congress created the Olympic Coast National Marine Sanctuary, but left open the questions of how large its boundaries should be and what activities should be permitted within it. At this writing, the National Oceanic and Atmospheric Administration (NOAA), is still puzzling over those questions, and environmentalists say the problems have more to do with politics than with what's best for the creatures who live out there. My dictionary defines a sanctuary as "a reservation where animals or birds are sheltered ... and may not be hunted or otherwise molested," but this definition is apparently not the government's: national marine sanctuaries elsewhere permit oil-drilling, commercial fishing, and a wide range of other activities, including the explosion of military armaments. Sea Lion Rock, south of the park boundary and offshore of the Copalis River, is bombed regularly by the U.S. Navy, which denies scientists' charges that the resident seabirds are harmed.

Most environmentalists want the sanctuary boundaries placed up to forty miles out to sea, and say that the area should be off-limits to both oil rigs and tankers. Environmentalists also say that U.S. and Canadian authorities should tighten regulations in the Strait of Juan de Fuca, which would lie beyond the sanctuary's boundaries. The Strait is the second-busiest shipping lane (after

Hong Kong) in the world, and up to seven hundred ships sail through it every day at full speed in weather famed for its inclemency; between 1975 and 1991, twenty-three collided, and near-misses are said to be frequent. Better ship-traffic rules would probably have prevented the 1988 and 1991 oil spills, but the multinational shipping industry doesn't feel it needs further regulation.

So we can expect more oil spills, more dead nature on the beaches. After each catastrophe, the tide pools and the birds and the animals die off by the unknown thousands. They gradually come back, but they don't come back to where they were before. The biologists say that if the seabird colonies keep getting inundated with oil spills every few years, they will eventually be unable to recover. Everything is connected, on the coast and everywhere else. Nature is a house of cards. Pull out too many, or the wrong one, and the flutter of falling cards sounds like the soft thrashing of a dying bird.

Real nature is pretty much gone now. What's left are a few places, such as the Olympic Coast, that look a lot like real nature, but aren't. Even the Antarctic ice holds traces of toxic chemicals, and marine biologists think some species of fish in Chilean waters are going blind because of the South Pole ozone hole. We have pretty much decided to go on burning fossil fuels—oil, gas, coal—and doing that will bump the planet's thermostat up a few more notches.

Scientists aren't arguing any more about *whether* global warming and the greenhouse effect are happening; the hottest summers ever recorded all came in the 1980s. Tans are dangerous, and I had a friend who recently died a young and painful death, of melanoma. As I write this, soggy Seattle is having its first water shortage, due to runaway population growth and a thin snowpack from last winter. The tropical rain forests, which play a key role in the global climate, are half gone now; in Costa Rica, supposedly an eco-model for other developing nations, all the unprotected forest has been cut and they're starting to log the wildlife refuges. In Zimbabwe, thousands of elephants and zebras are being slaughtered to feed the rapidly expanding numbers of drought-starved people.

Global warming is coming, even if we shut down all the polluting industries and stop driving our cars right now. Now the scientists are just arguing about how bad it's going to be. They run their theories out into the future on big computers; they get back wildly differing answers. One big change is going to be that the warming climate will melt some of the polar ice and the sea level will rise, perhaps as little as three feet higher in the next few decades; but it could be ten feet, maybe more. The coastal cities will have to do some very expensive remodeling.

Next to that (and next to drought, crop failure, and other catastrophes we can only guess at), what will happen to the Olympic Coast will not cause widespread concern. Hotter summers and less rainfall will not be good for the forests and the wildlife. The plants and animals in the intertidal zone, for example, depend on a very narrow range of temperatures. The higher sea level will start moving the beaches back perhaps a football-field's length within the next few decades, and will cover some picturesque rocks. The change will be gradual, maybe even unnoticeable, unless you start counting the anemone in a certain patch of tide pools every summer and keep a record.

In *The End of Nature*, Bill McKibben concludes that, "Though not in our time, and not in the time of our children, or their children, if we now, *today* [his emphasis], limited our numbers and our desires and our ambitions, perhaps nature could someday resume its independent working. Perhaps the temperature could someday adjust itself to its own setting, and the rain fall of its own accord."

So we are left with a kind of hope, finally. Not hope that any politician will be brave enough to make a difference. Not hope that if we drive our cars less, global warming won't happen. Not hope that you will live to see the salmon crowd the rivers again, or the tree farms become ancient forests.

Instead, we must hope that nature will "someday resume its independent working." Hope that somewhere off in the distant future, enlightened humans will survive whatever it is that's coming. Hope that they will love both the sea and the seacoast, that its rocky, ragged borders will have real forests and eagles and anemones, and a pervasive sense of mystery. Hope that those people then will lift their eyes joyously to distant blue horizons, and go walking with the whales.

Bibliography

General

Carson, Rachel. *The Edge of the Sea*. Boston: Houghton Mifflin Co., 1955.

———. *The Sea Around Us*. New York: Oxford University Press, 1951.

Kirk, Ruth. *The Olympic Seashore*. Seattle: Pacific Northwest National Parks Association, Inc., 1962.

Steelquist, Robert U. *Washington's Coast*. Helena, Mont.: American Geographic Publishing, 1987.

Strickland, Richard, and Daniel Jack Chasan. *Coastal Washington: A Synthesis of Information*. Seattle: Washington Sea Grant Program, University of Washington, 1989.

Warren, Henry C. *Olympic: The Story Behind the Scenery*. Las Vegas, Nev.: KC Publications, 1982.

Birds

Dawson, William Leon. *The Birds of Washington*. Seattle: The Occidental Publishing Co., 1909.

Speich, Steven M. and Terence R. Wahl. *Catalog of Washington Seabird Colonies*. Washington, D.C.: U.S. Department of the Interior, Fish and Wildlife Service, 1989.

Udvardy, Miklos D. F. *The Audubon Society Field Guide to North American Birds, Western Region*. New York: Alfred A. Knopf, 1977.

Geology

Rau, Weldon W. *Geology of the Washington Coast between Point Grenville and the Hoh River*. Washington State Department of Natural Resources, 1973.

———. *Washington Coastal Geology between the Hoh and Quillayute Rivers*. Washington State Department of Natural Resources, 1980.

History

Andrews, Ralph. *Indian Primitive*. Seattle: Superior Publishing Co., 1960.

Drucker, P. *Indians of the Northwest Coast*. Garden City, N.Y.: The Natural History Press, 1963.

Gibbs, James. *Shipwrecks of the Pacific Coast*. Portland: Binfords & Mort, 1962.

Kirk, Ruth and Carmela Alexander. *Exploring Washington's Past*. Seattle and London: University of Washington Press, 1990.

Lien, Carsten. *Olympic Battleground*. San Francisco: Sierra Club Books, 1991.

Intertidal

Kozloff, E. *Seashore Life of the Northern Pacific Coast*. Seattle and London: University of Washington Press, 1983.

Wertheim, Anne. *The Intertidal Wilderness*. San Francisco: Sierra Club Books, 1984.

Whales

Haley, Delphine, ed. *Marine Mammals*. Seattle: Pacific Search Press, 1978.

Oceanic Society. *Field Guide to the Gray Whale*. Seattle: Sasquatch Books, 1989.

Index

About the Author

A lifelong Pacific Northwesterner, Seattle writer David Hooper has published award-winning articles on environmental issues, science, nature, and foreign travel in a wide variety of magazines and newspapers. He and his wife Candace are avid backpackers and cross-country skiers.

THE MOUNTAINEERS, founded in 1906, is a nonprofit outdoor activity and conservation club, whose mission is "to explore, study, preserve, and enjoy the natural beauty of the outdoors...." Based in Seattle, Washington, the club is now the third-largest such organization in the United States, with 12,000 members and four branches throughout Washington State.

The Mountaineers sponsors both classes and year-round outdoor activities in the Pacific Northwest, which include hiking, mountain climbing, ski-touring, snowshoeing, bicycling, camping, kayaking and canoeing, nature study, sailing, and adventure travel. The club's conservation division supports environmental causes through educational activities, sponsoring legislation, and presenting informational programs. All club activities are led by skilled, experienced volunteers, who are dedicated to promoting safe and responsible enjoyment and preservation of the outdoors.

The Mountaineers Books, an active, nonprofit publishing program of the club, produces guidebooks, instructional texts, historical works, natural history guides, and works on environmental conservation. All books produced by The Mountaineers are aimed at fulfilling the club's mission.

If you would like to participate in these organized outdoor activities or the club's programs, consider a membership in The Mountaineers. For information and an application, write or call The Mountaineers, Club Headquarters, 300 Third Avenue West, Seattle, Washington 98119; (206) 284-6310.

Send or call for our catalog of more than 200 outdoor books:

The Mountaineers Books
1011 SW Klickitat Way, Suite 107
Seattle, WA 98134
1-800-553-4453